NakedComix

THE REAL ADULT COLORING BOOK

BY JAMES COURTNEY

I0473599

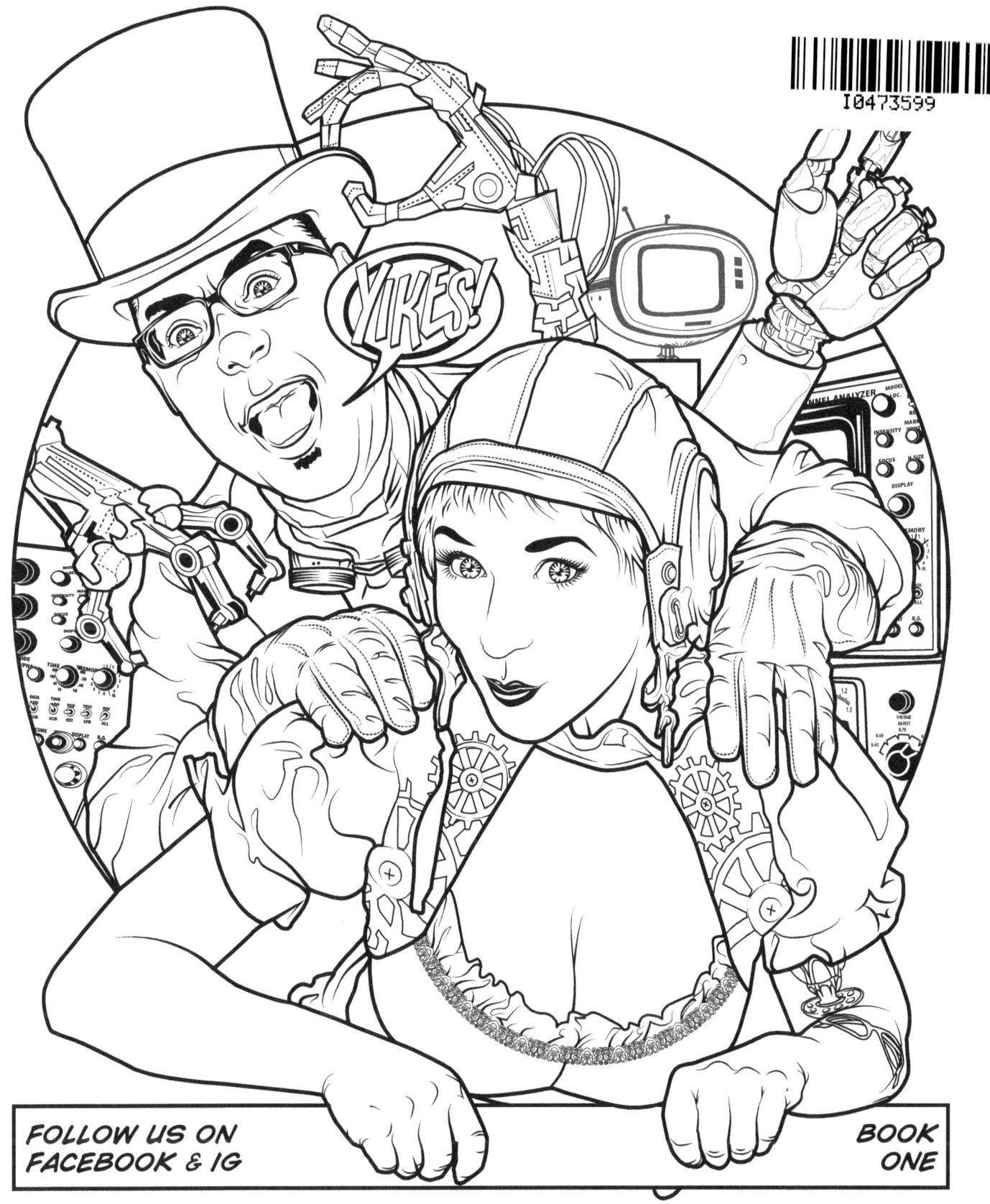

FOLLOW US ON
FACEBOOK & IG

BOOK
ONE

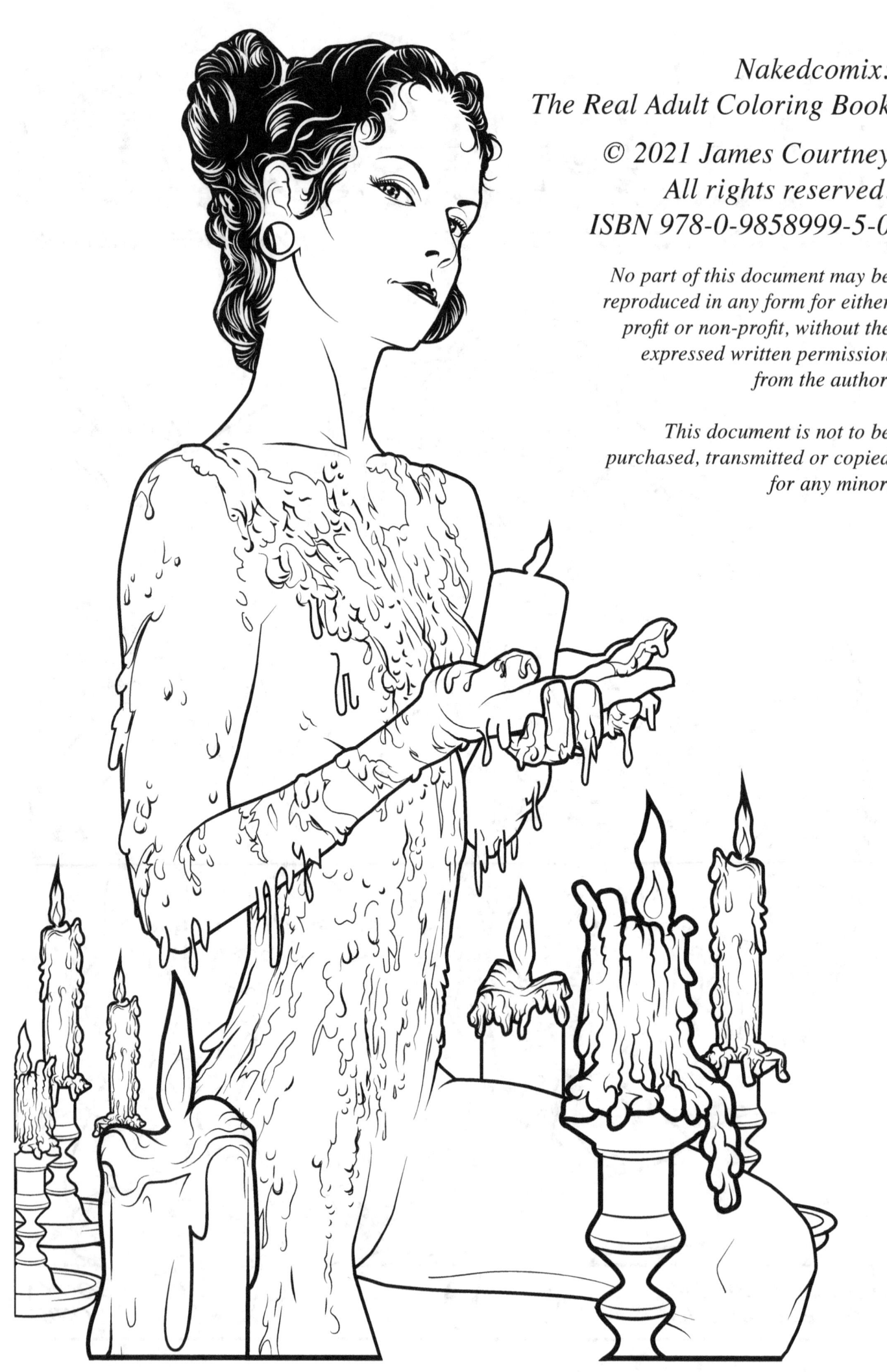

Nakedcomix:
The Real Adult Coloring Book

© 2021 James Courtney
All rights reserved.
ISBN 978-0-9858999-5-0

There's a party in James Courtney's head and you are invited to join. And what a party it is--Courtney's style is distinctive, bold and instantly recognizable. The people in his books have an energy that seems to literally pop off the pages in an endless variety. From burlesque dancers to fetishists to fire-eaters, the body types, styles and types of play are a wide ranging and unexpected buffet all gathered together under James's lens.

An early love of both photography and comic books gelled together to create what is now an ongoing series of adult coloring books with a focus on kink, burlesque and all of the varied and sexy ways that adults find to play. Starting with a camera in high school borrowed from his father and documenting the friends and events around him, James eventually found himself in art school, where he studied illustration.

An art school background with a focus on illustration led a comics loving James to realize what many comic books are missing...a sense of realism and authentic, honest joy. Without actual models to base your art off of, an artist will, consciously or unconsciously, tend to pick the same body types drawn through their own personal lens. Bodies can become unrealistic and repetitive if an artist stays in their comfort zone. James was determined to remedy that and sought to do more inclusive art. One thing led to another and in 2012 the adult coloring books so many of us know and love first came into being.

What makes Courtney's work so distinctive is the steps taken in order to make it--after a traditional photoshoot is done, the images are then subjected to the Courtney treatment and turned into the black and white drawings of what we normally associate with coloring books. Knowing that the photoshoots are destined to eventually become broader line drawing shifts the style and tone, with a focus on things that will translate more easily to the medium of coloring books.

In this case, very ADULT coloring books. But why should kids have all of the fun? Adults deserve coloring books too! Not to mention, it has been proven that the act of coloring can be a soothing and stress reducing activity. I don't know about you, but I am of the firm belief that stress reduction is something we can all use some more of.

Based on the continued demand of his coloring books (almost a decade now!), we do want to spend some time indulging in some sexy soothing self-care. So what are you waiting for? Grab a marker or some colored pencils and jump into James Courtney's world! I promise you won't be judged for coloring outside the lines. Heck, you don't even have to color this hot little volume if you don't want to. Just enjoying the pictures is perfectly valid as well. There is no right or wrong way to do it. It's a party and you are holding the invitation in your hot little hands. Dive on in, the water is fine and the fun is about to begin.

Rain DeGrey is a noted sex educator, model, writer and co-host of the Dirty Talk Podcast. Visit her website, www.raindegrey.com

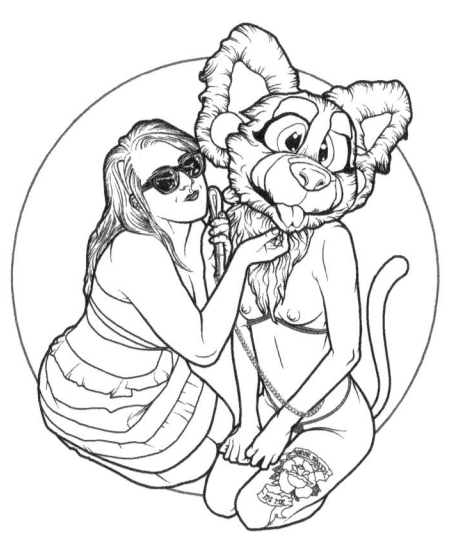

Cover Model: Kitty Meow
Front Page Models: Kingfish and
Alexa Von Kickenface
Left Model: Kitty Litterpaws
Right Models: Miss_Catonic & Kitty Litterpaws

Living Art

Model: Babraham Lincoln

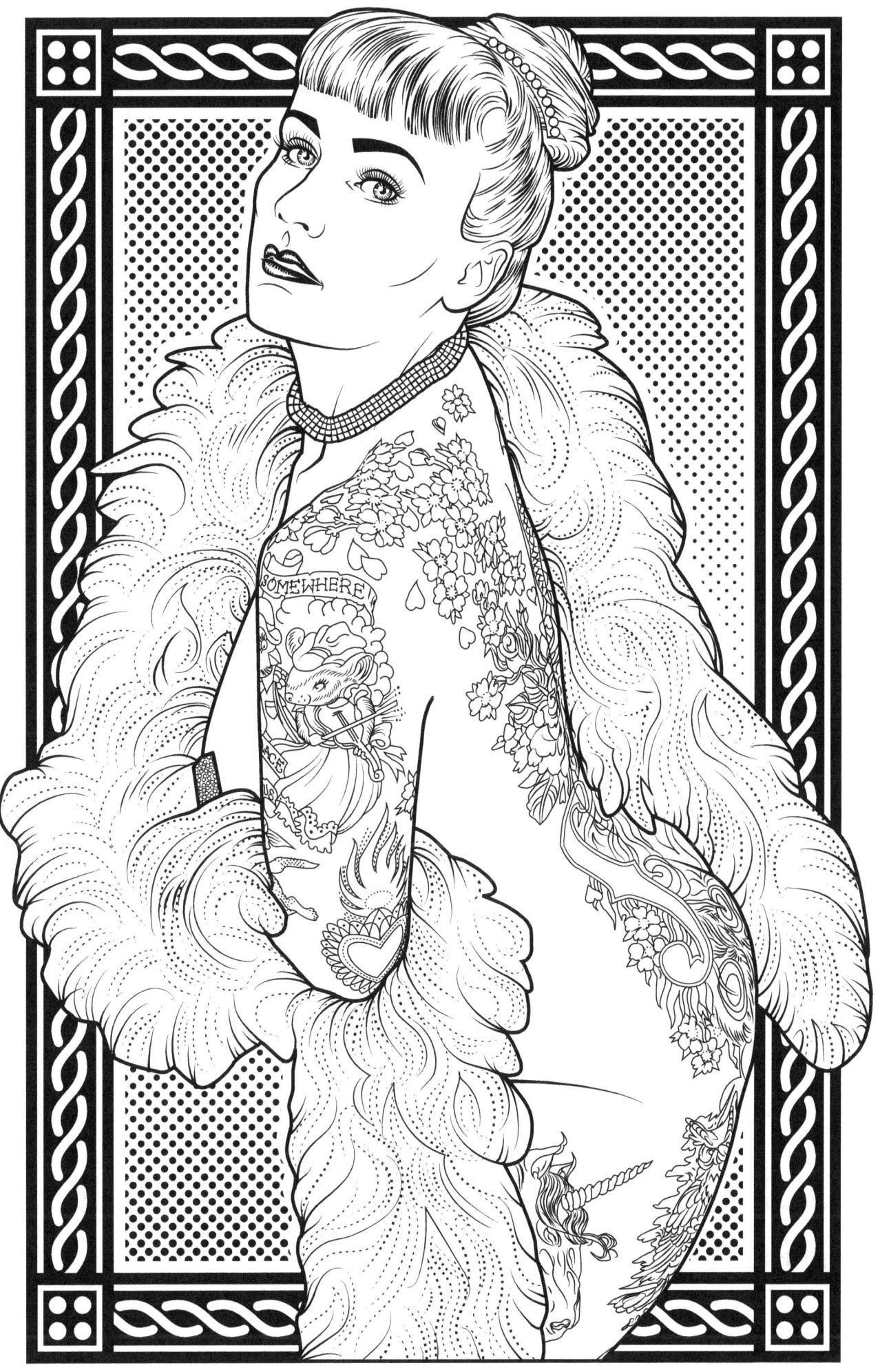

Fooling Around With Charlie D.

Model: Charlie Duneaux

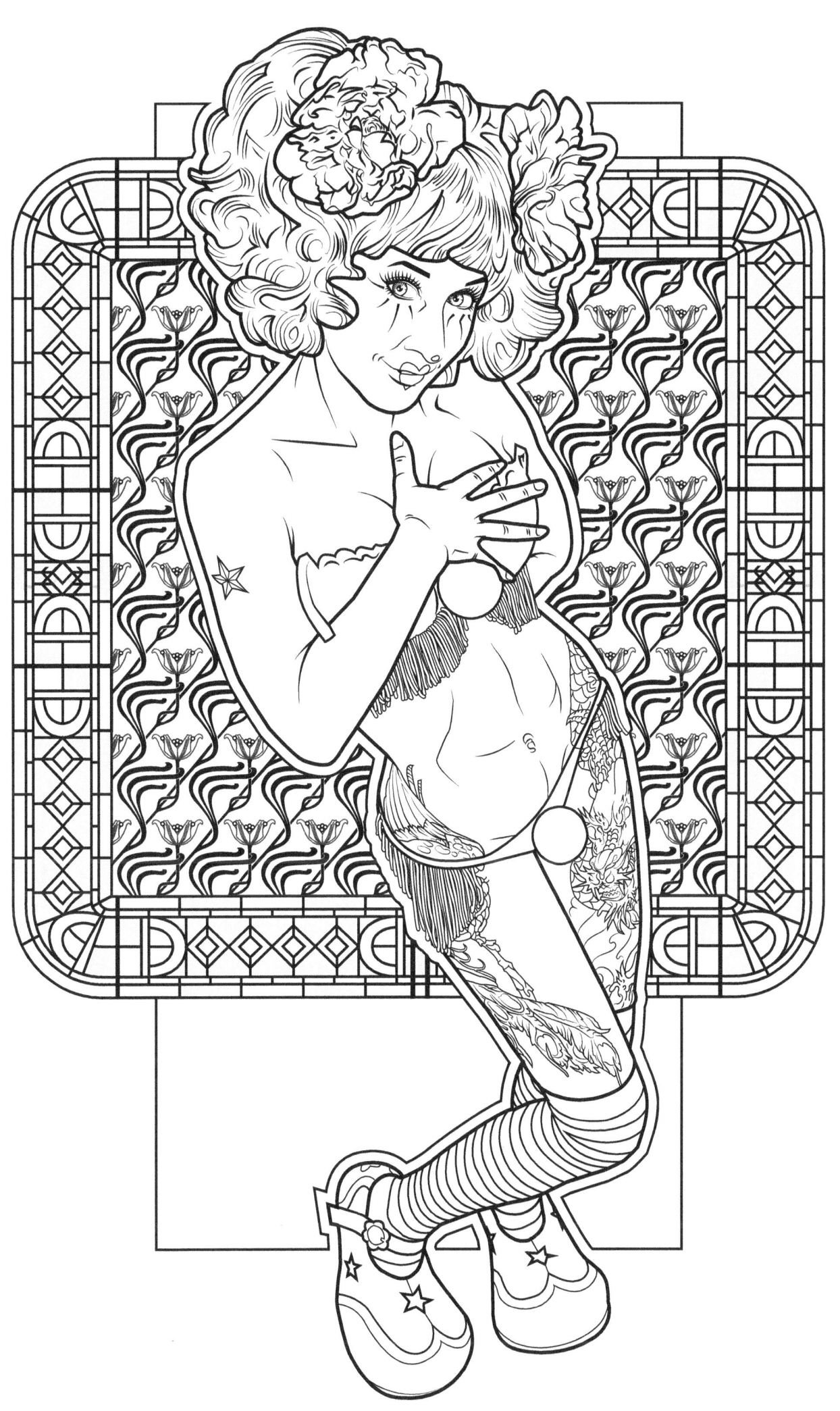

The Chairman

Model: Aurora Rose

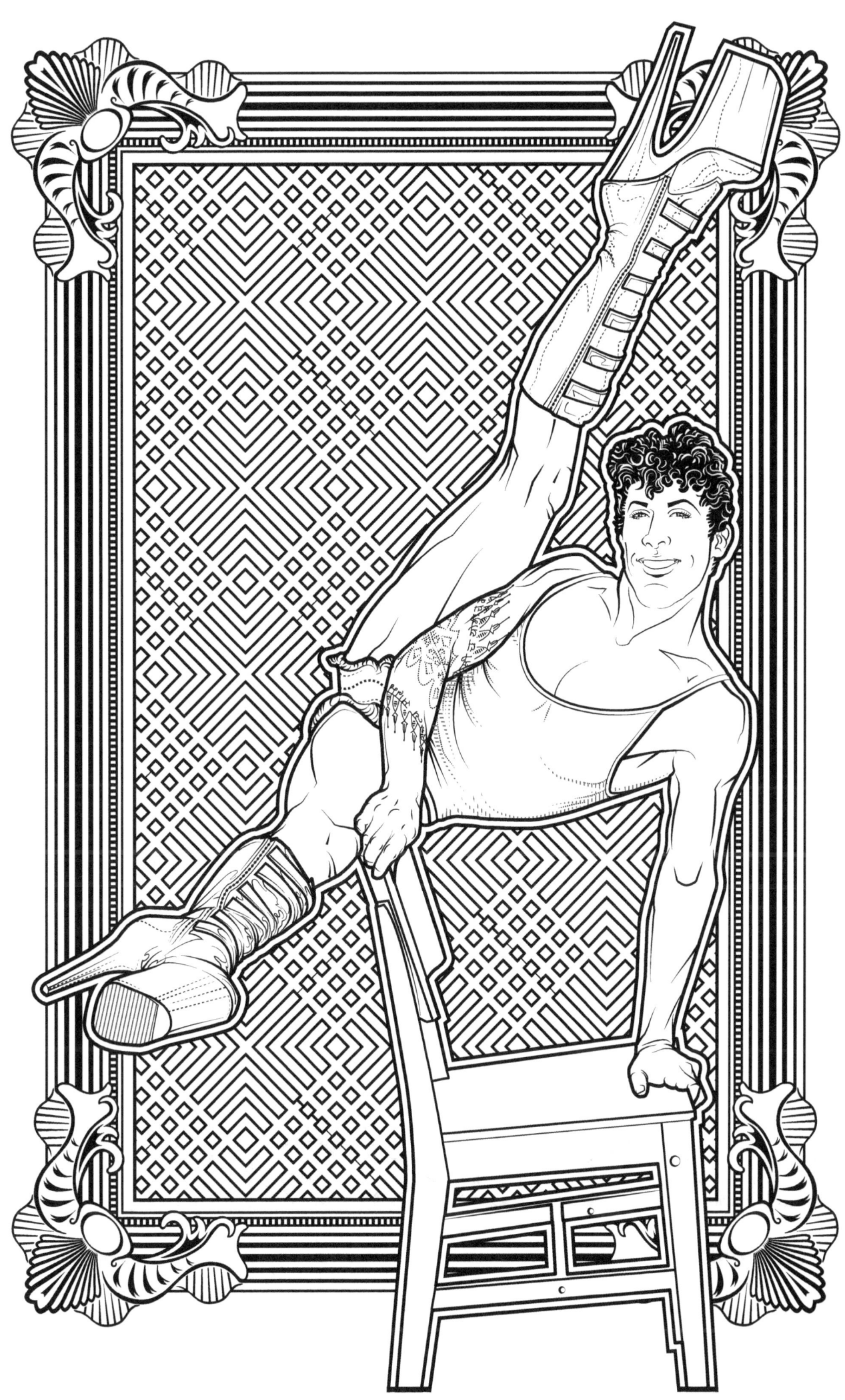

Daddy's Bad Girl

Model: Girlcub

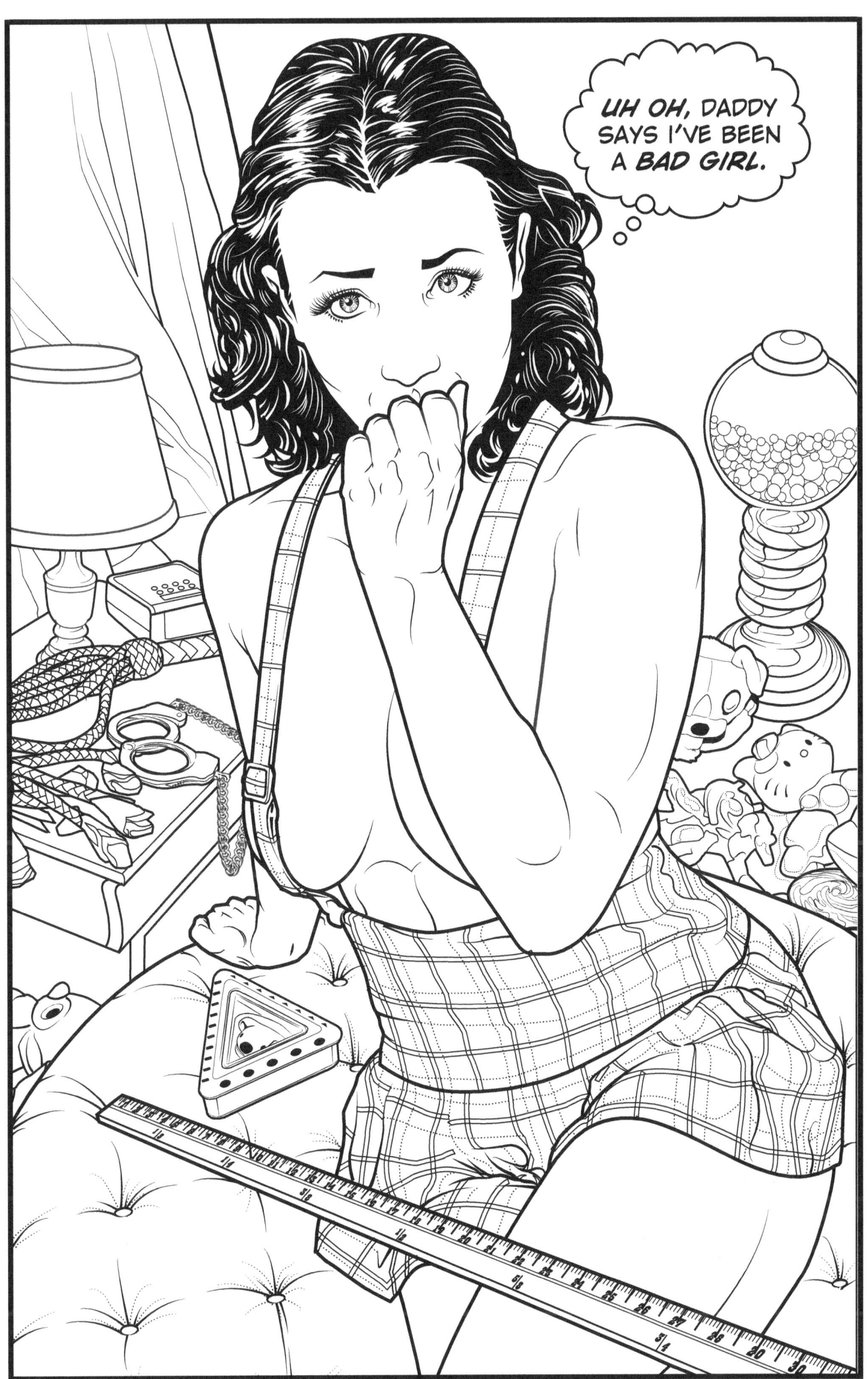

Chelsea In Latex

Model: Chelsea Christian, Latex Dress by Lust Designs

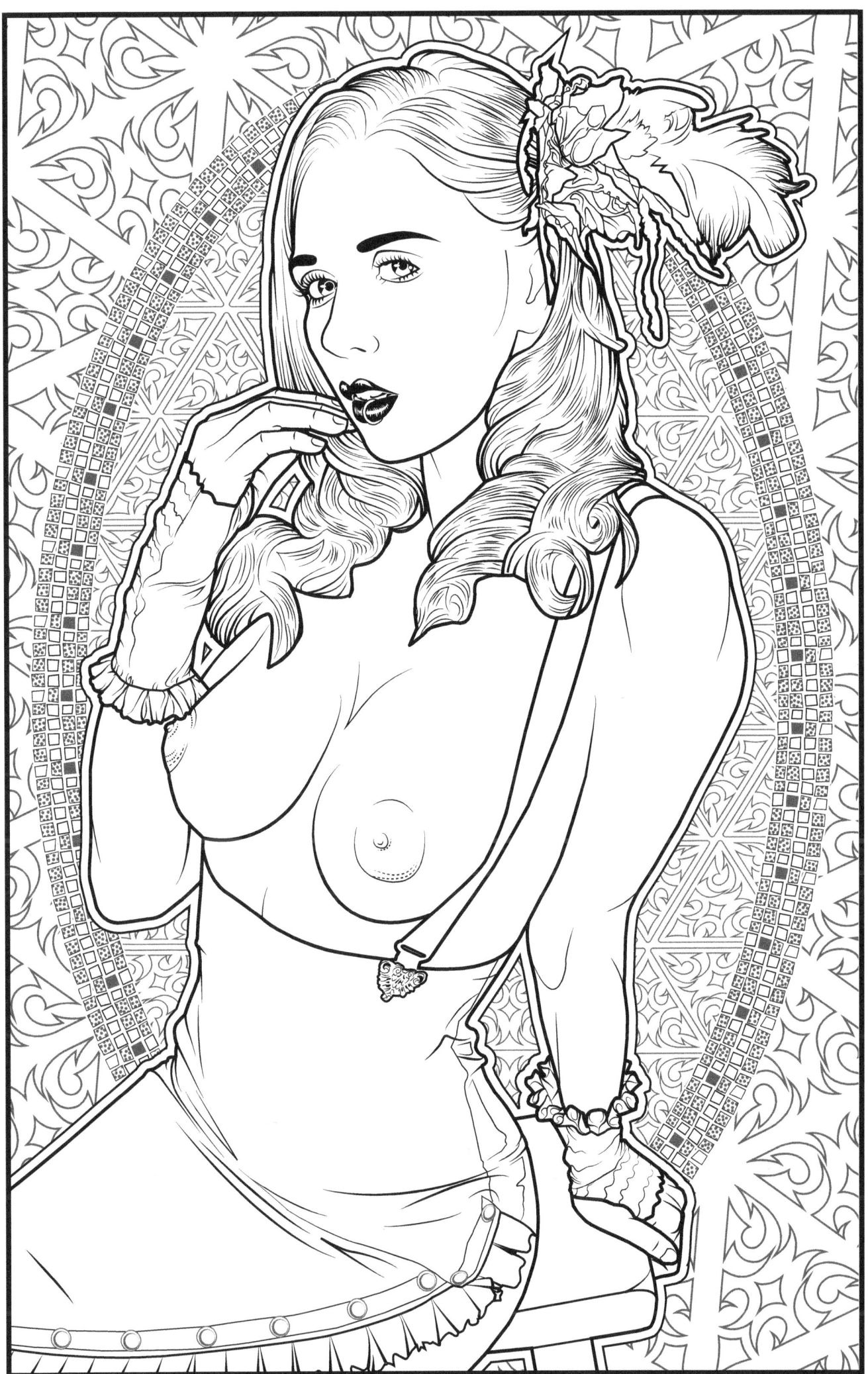

Summertime Fun

Model: Pixie Vanílle

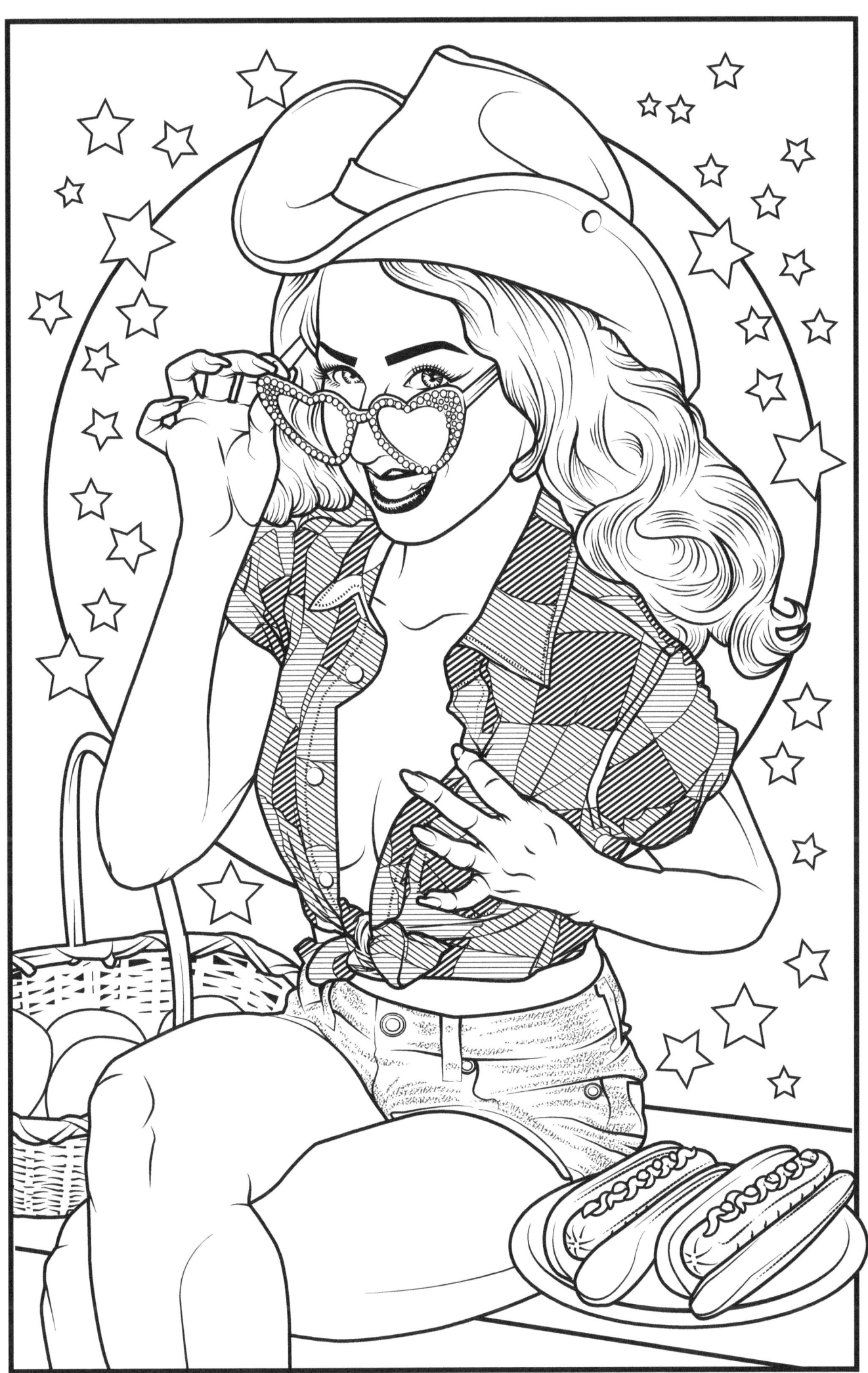

Cthulhu Dances

Model: Persephone Pon Farr

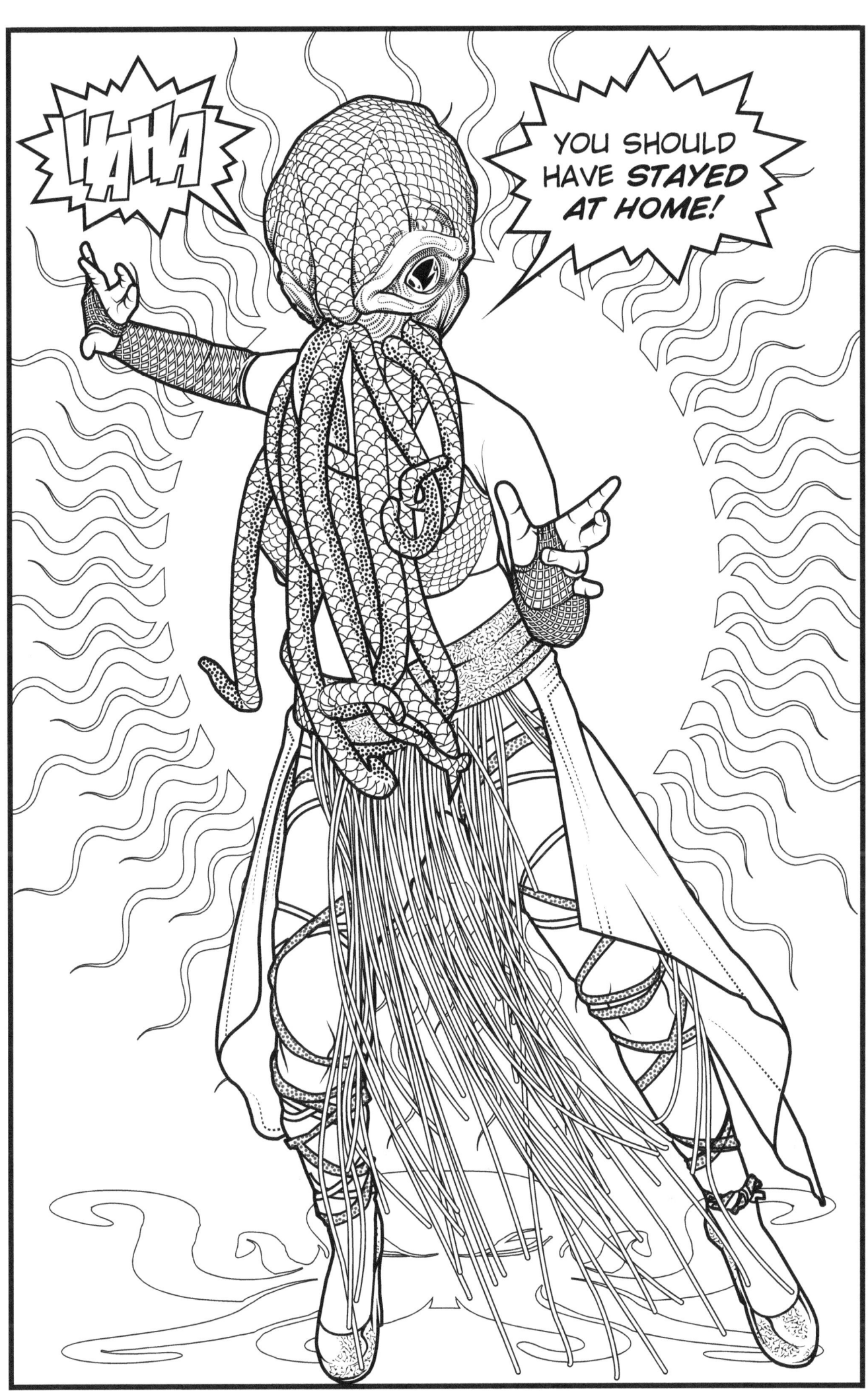

Classic Starlet

Model: Dorian Dietrich

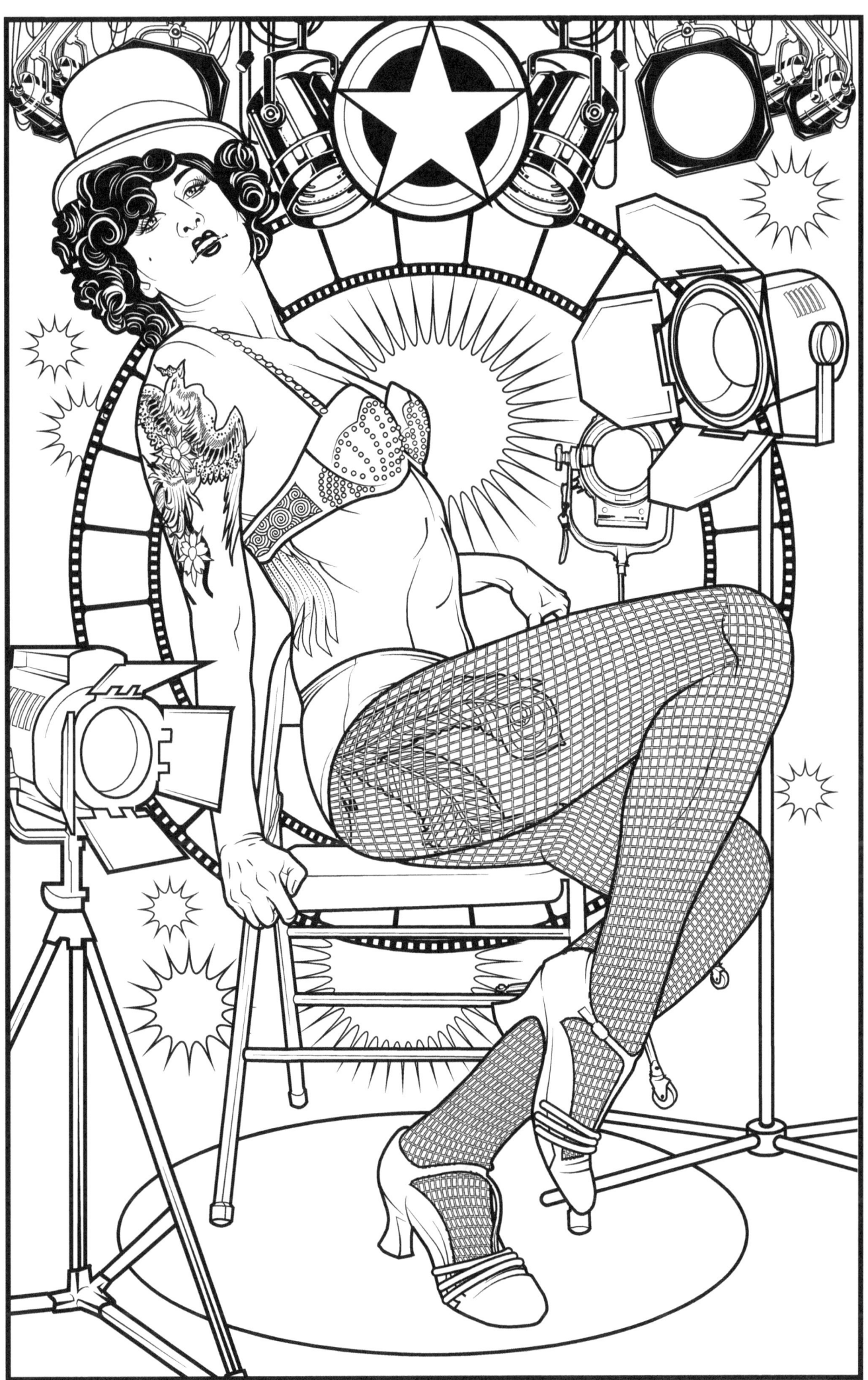

Pistols And Pasties

Model: JonBenet Butterbuns

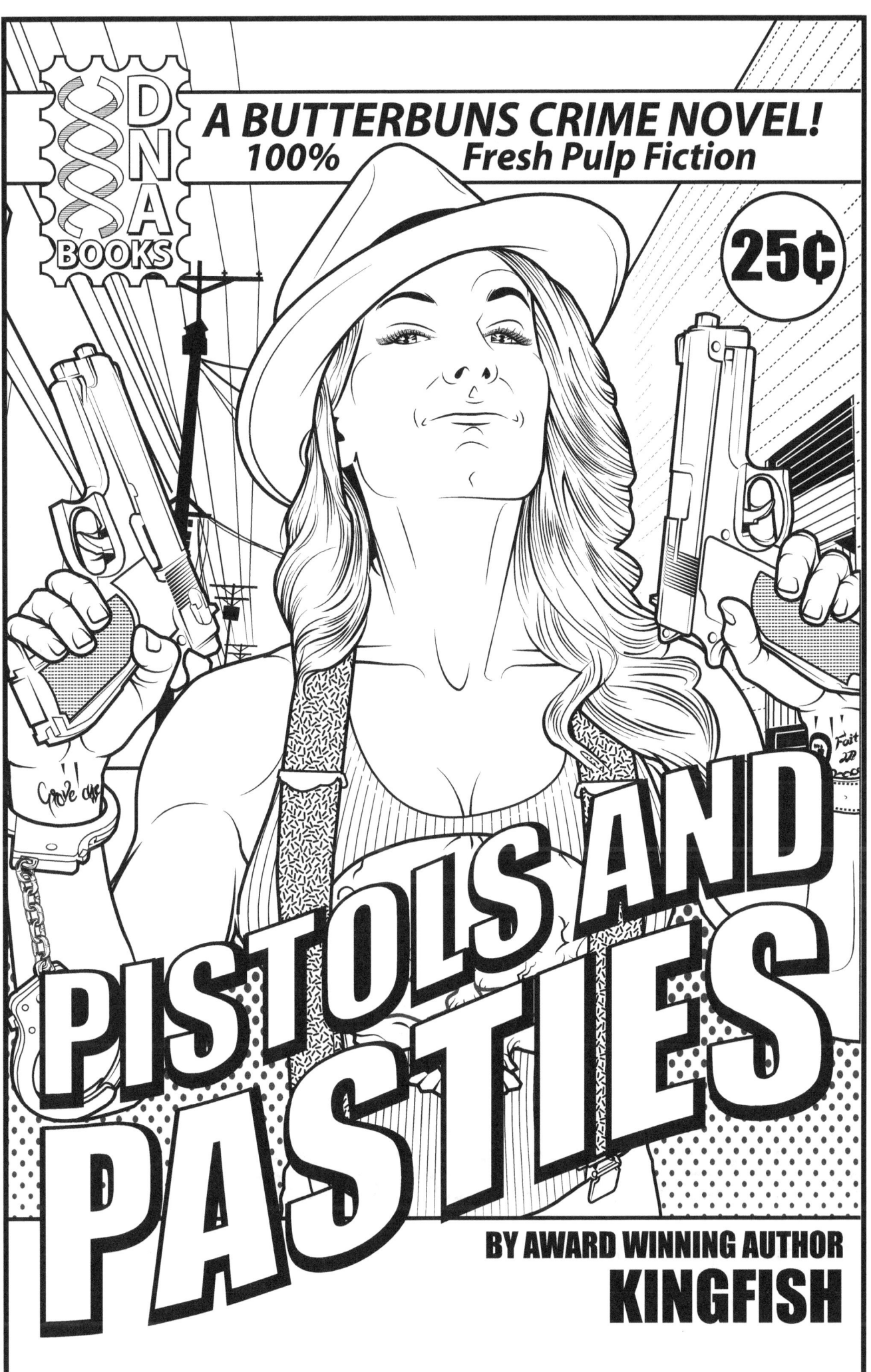

Amazing Grace

Model: Grace Bones

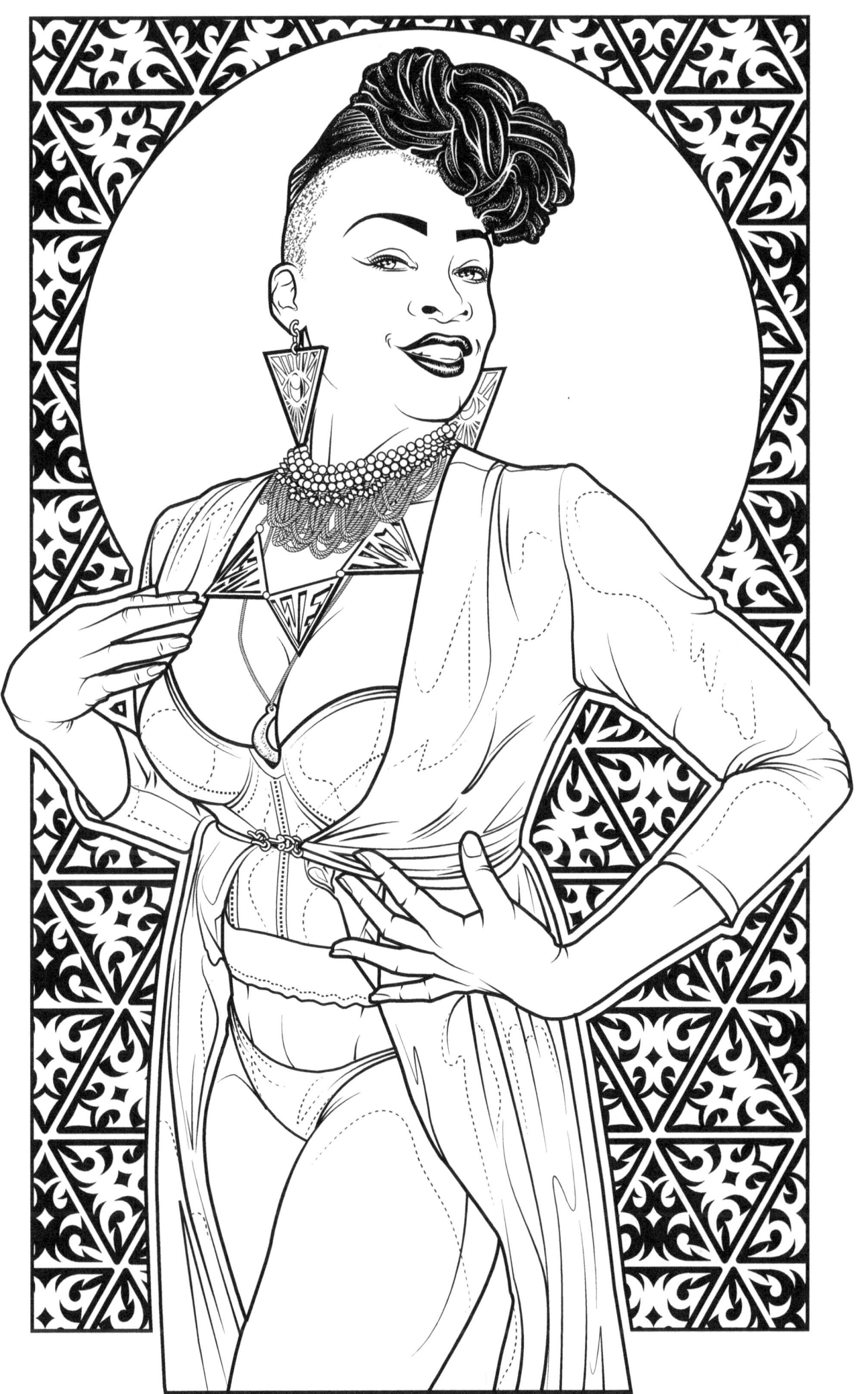

Highly Flammable

Model: Ivizia Dakini

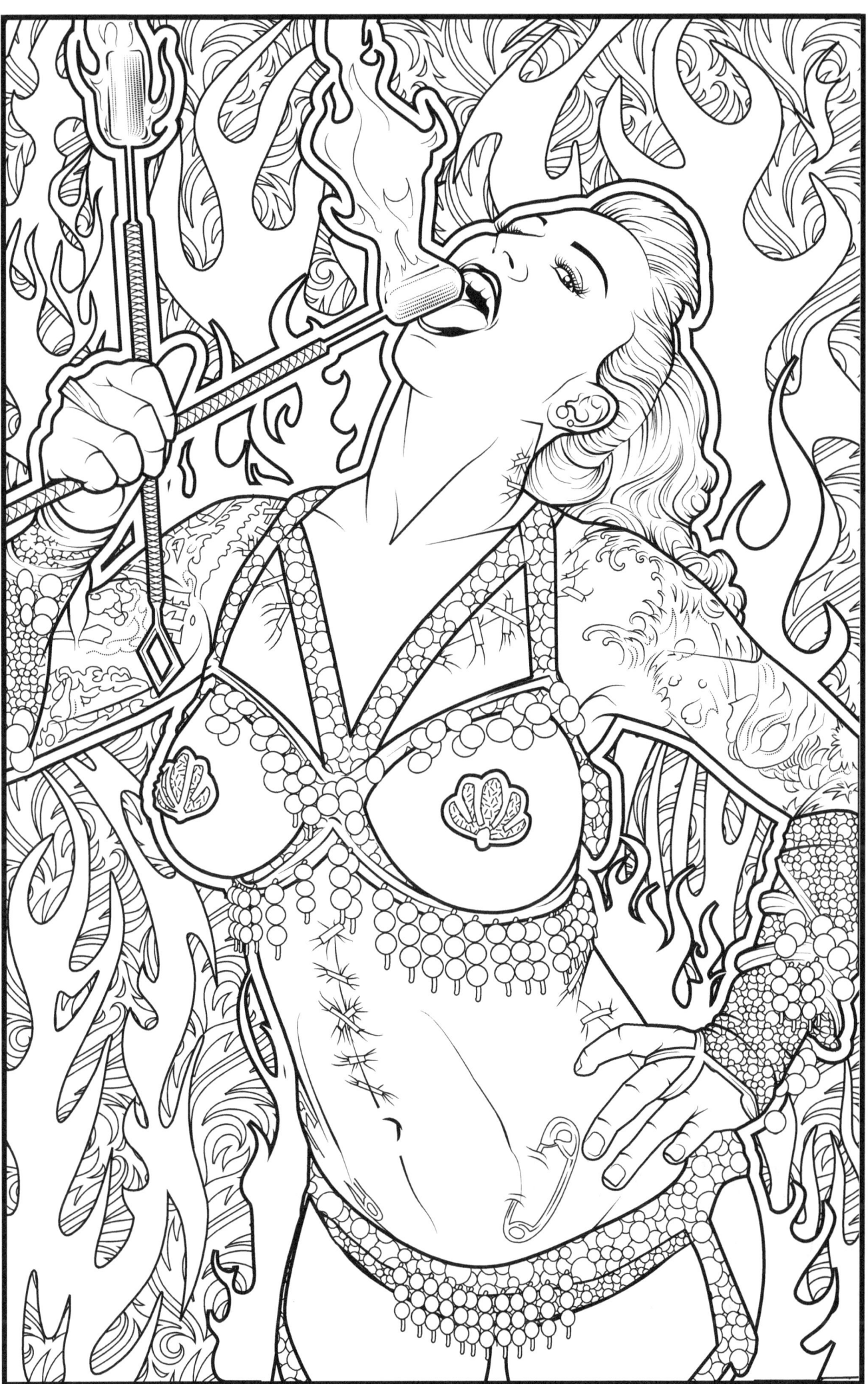

Jain's Attitude

Model: Jain Dowe,

Burlesque performer and producer of Apothecery Raree

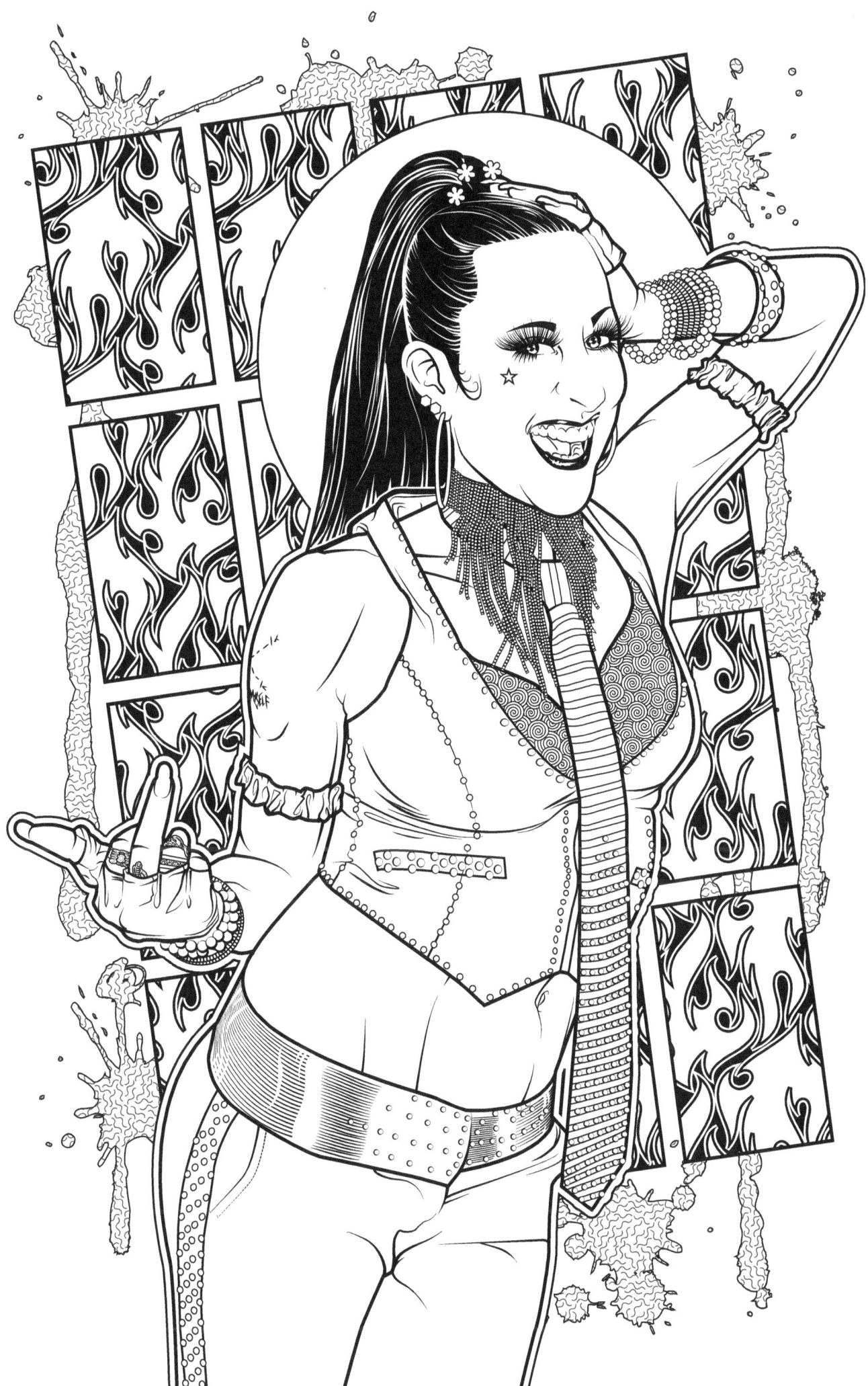

Kill Bill

Model: Sweet Belize

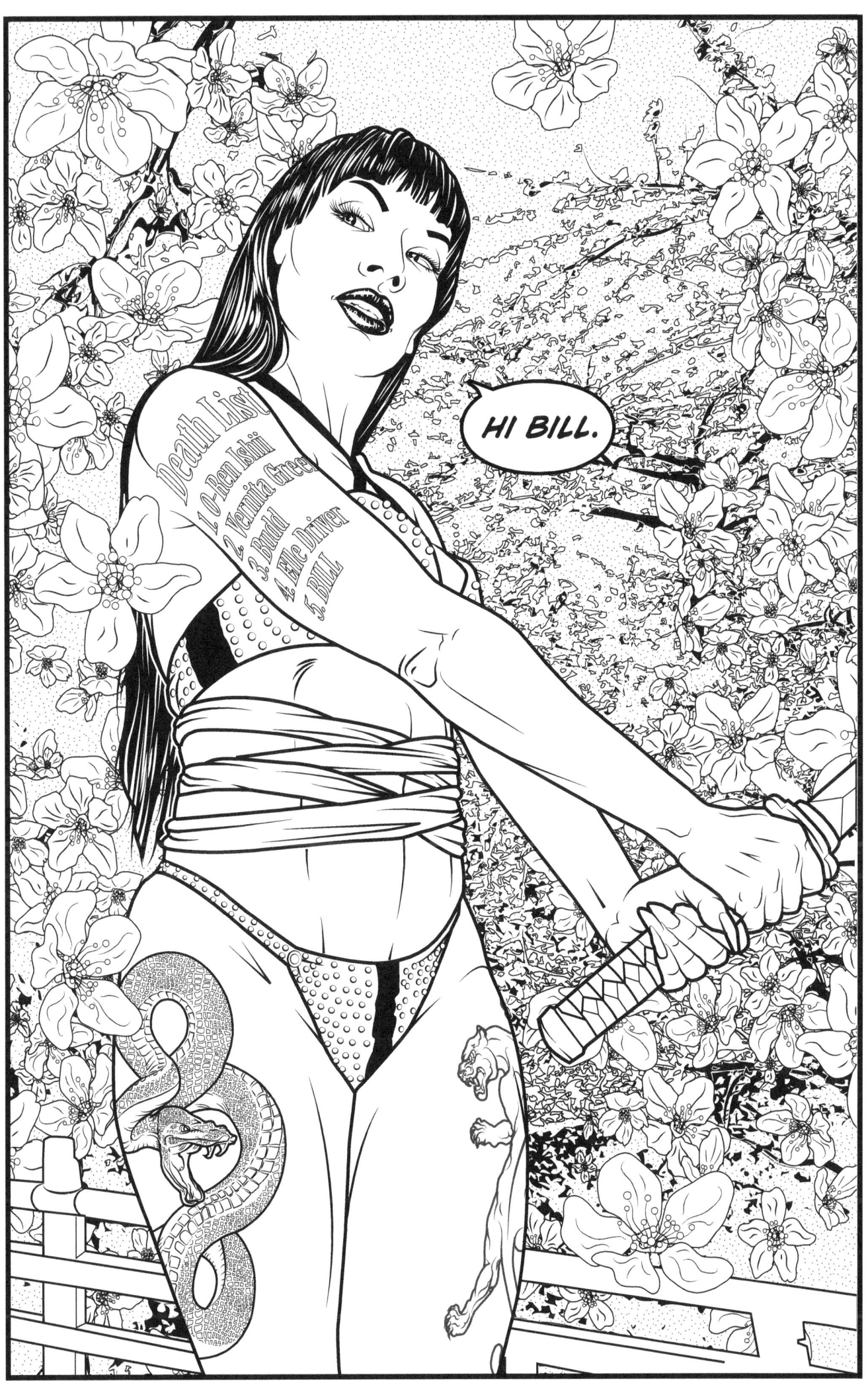

Killer Clara

Model: Clara Bodacious

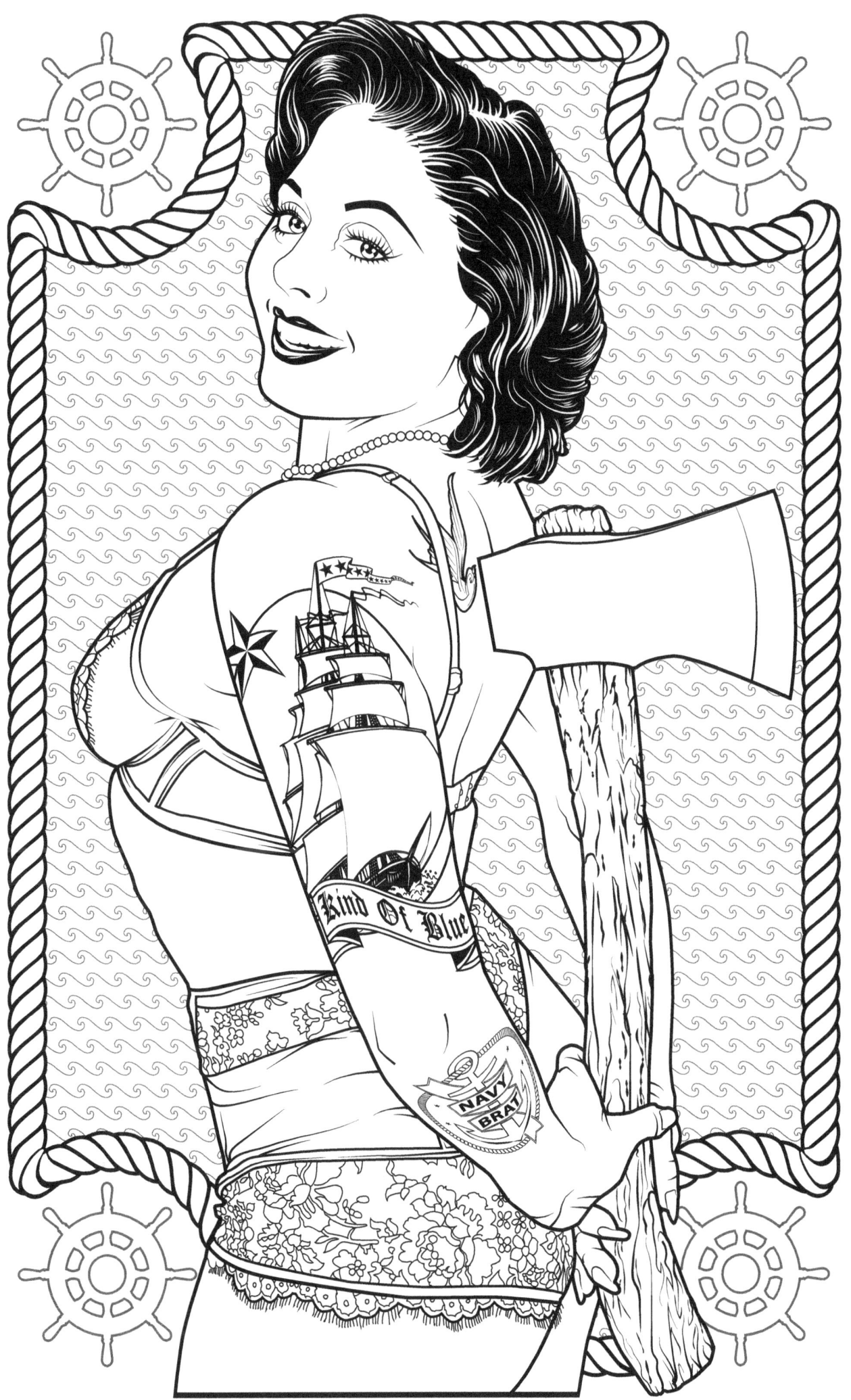

Who The Hell Are You?

Model: Lady Satan

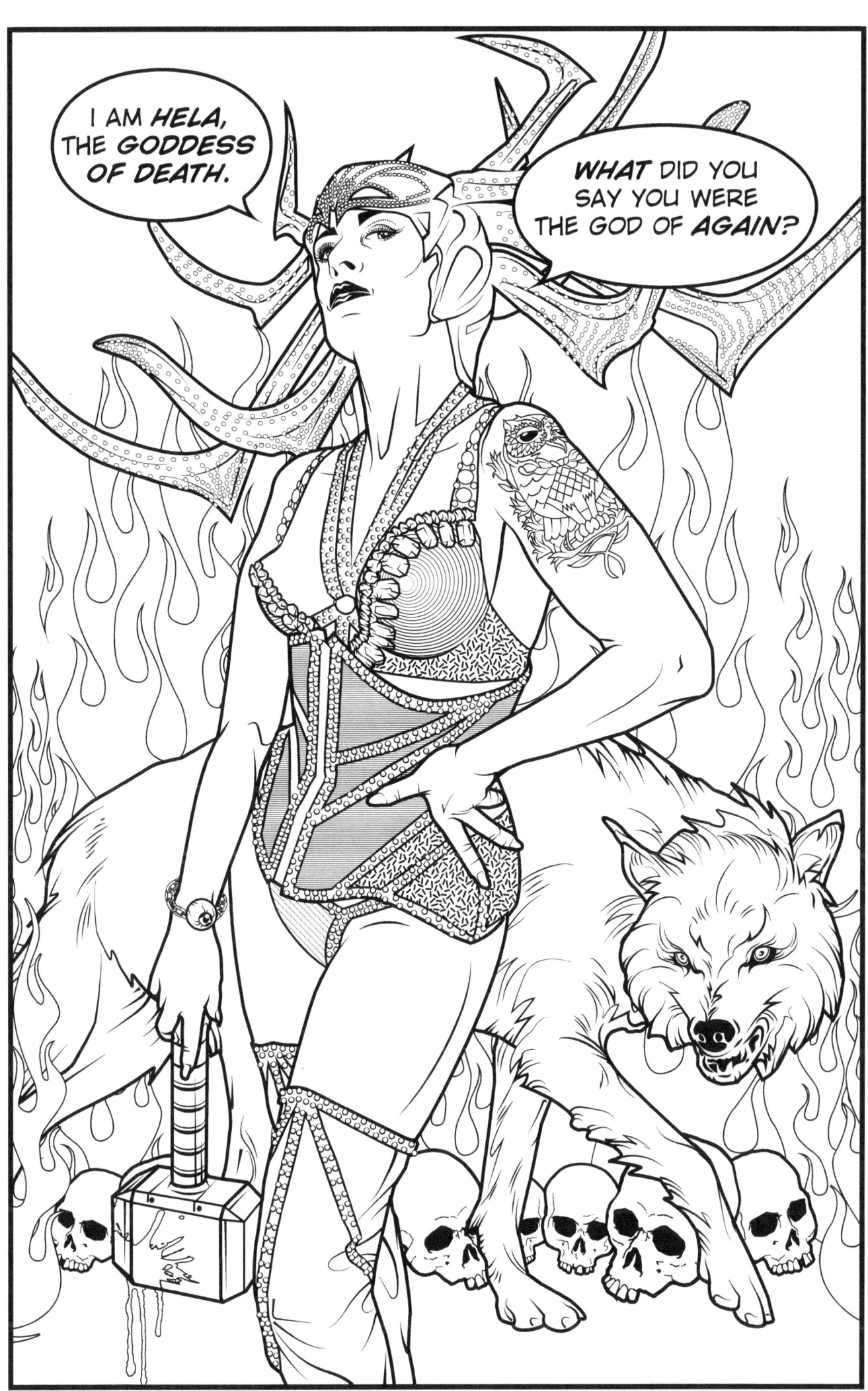

Ready For The Fireworks?

Model: Lusty Von Dame

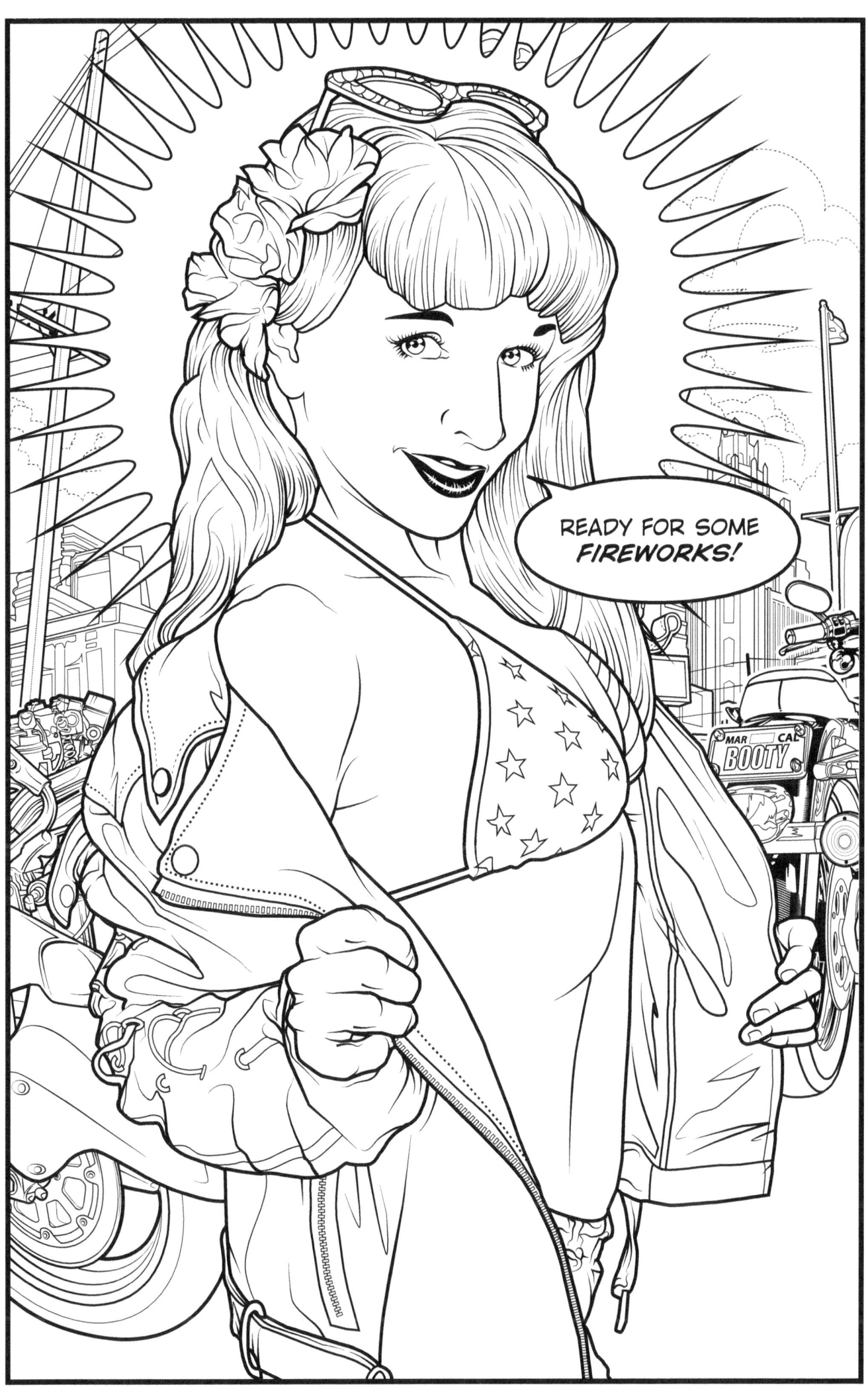

Outdoor Fun

Model: McKenna Holland

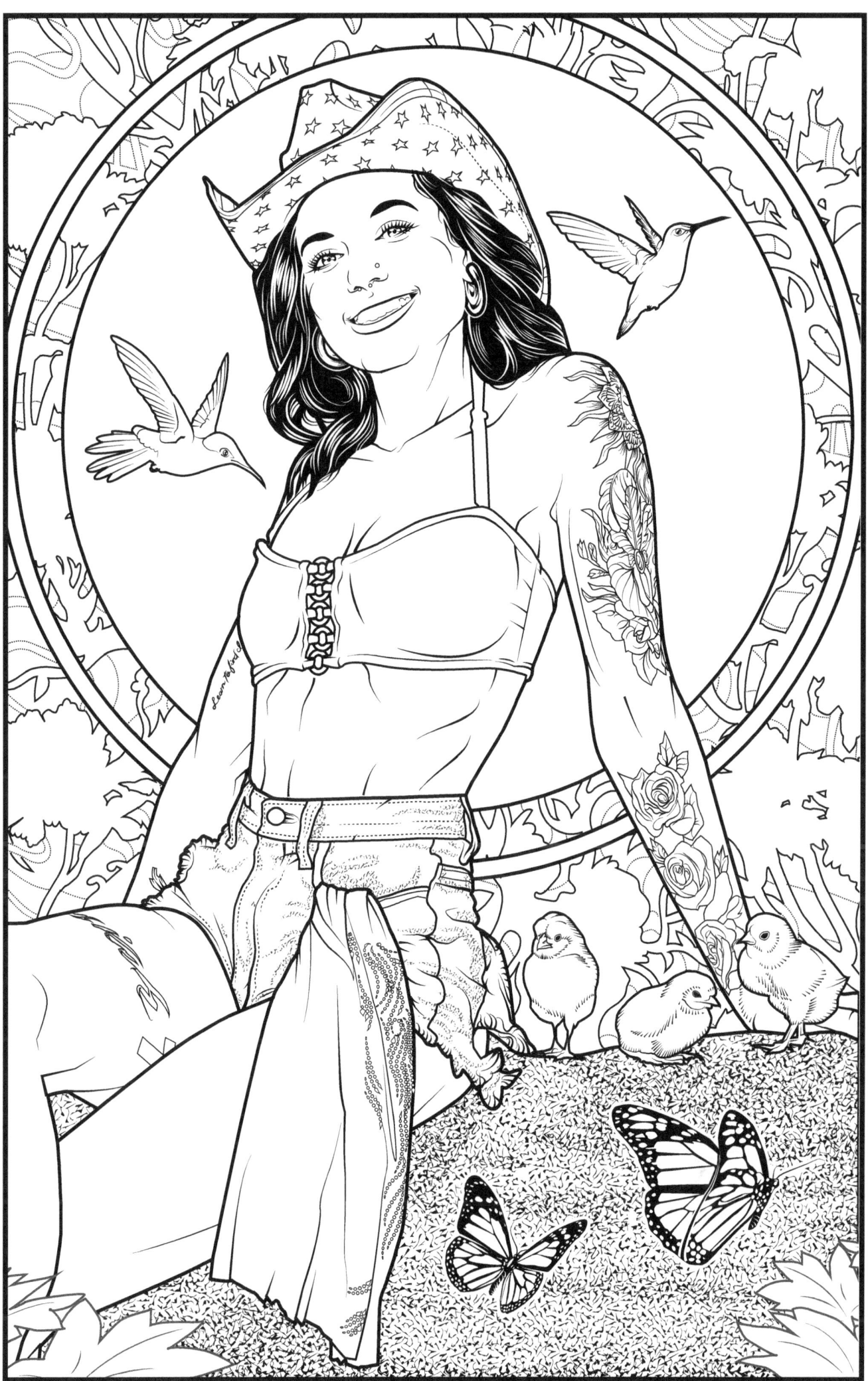

Dark Dreams

Models: Muza de la Luz

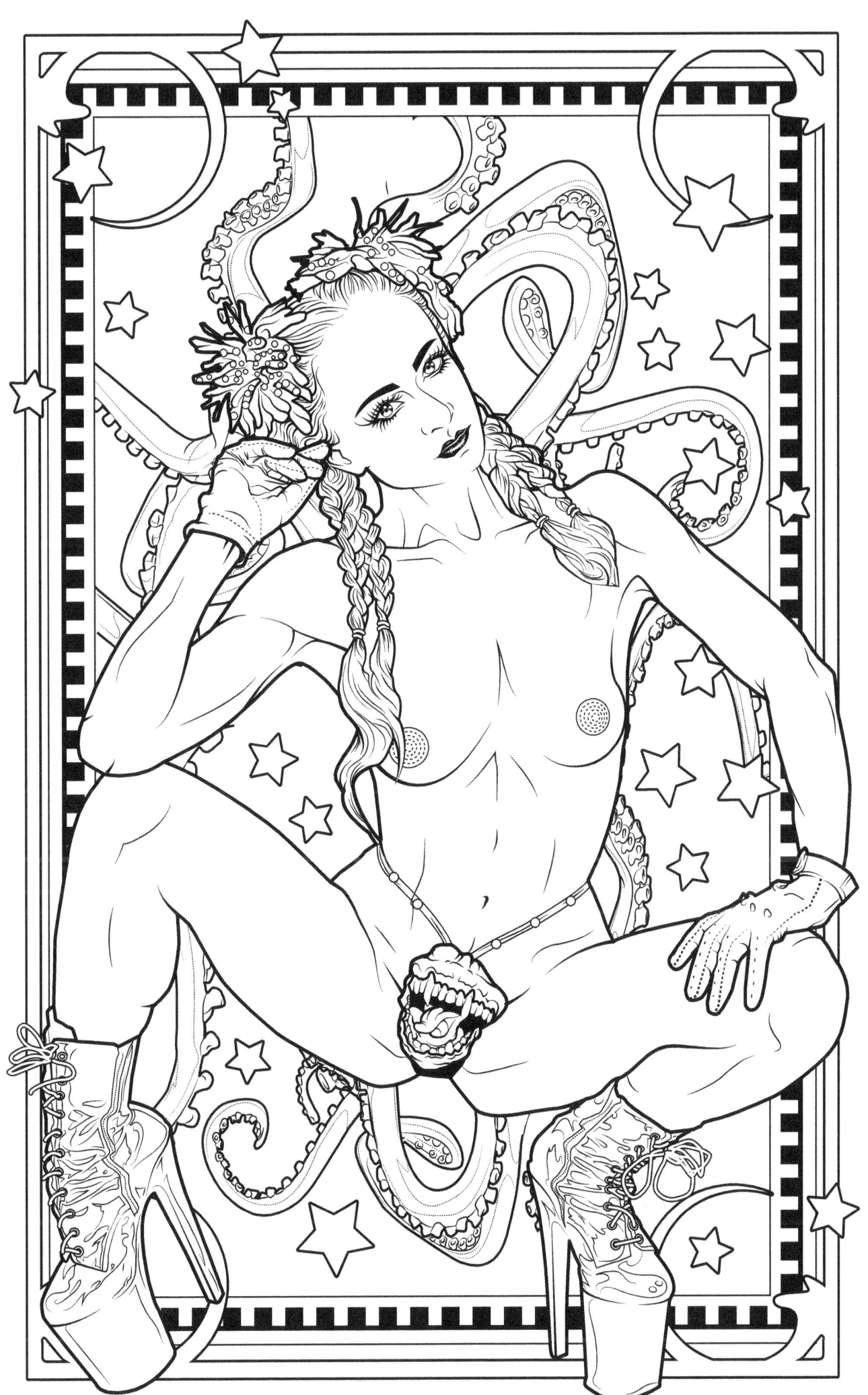

Radical Happiness

Model: Ivizia Dakini

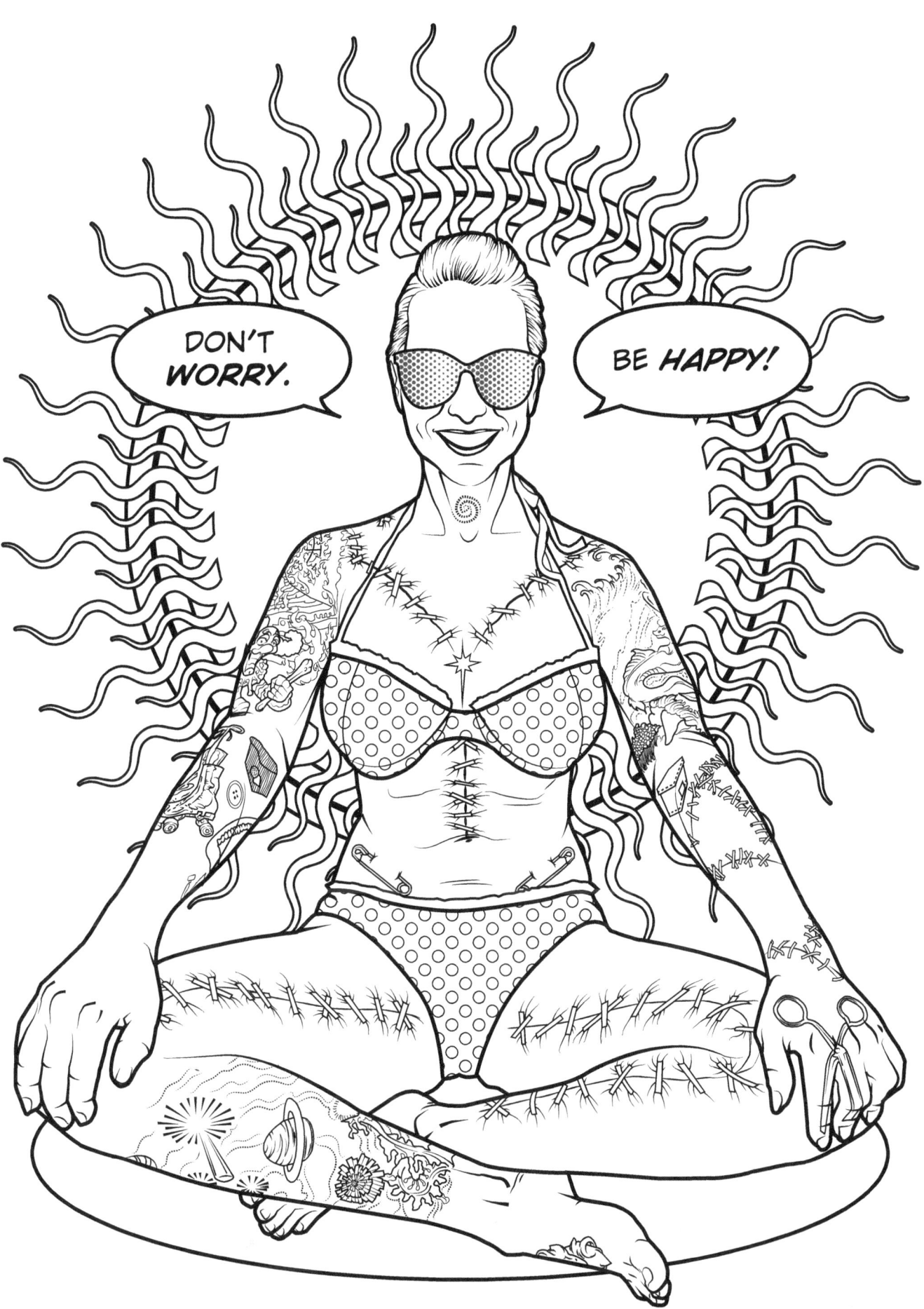

RADICAL HAPPINESS

Ready To Kick Ass

Model: Pixie Vanílle

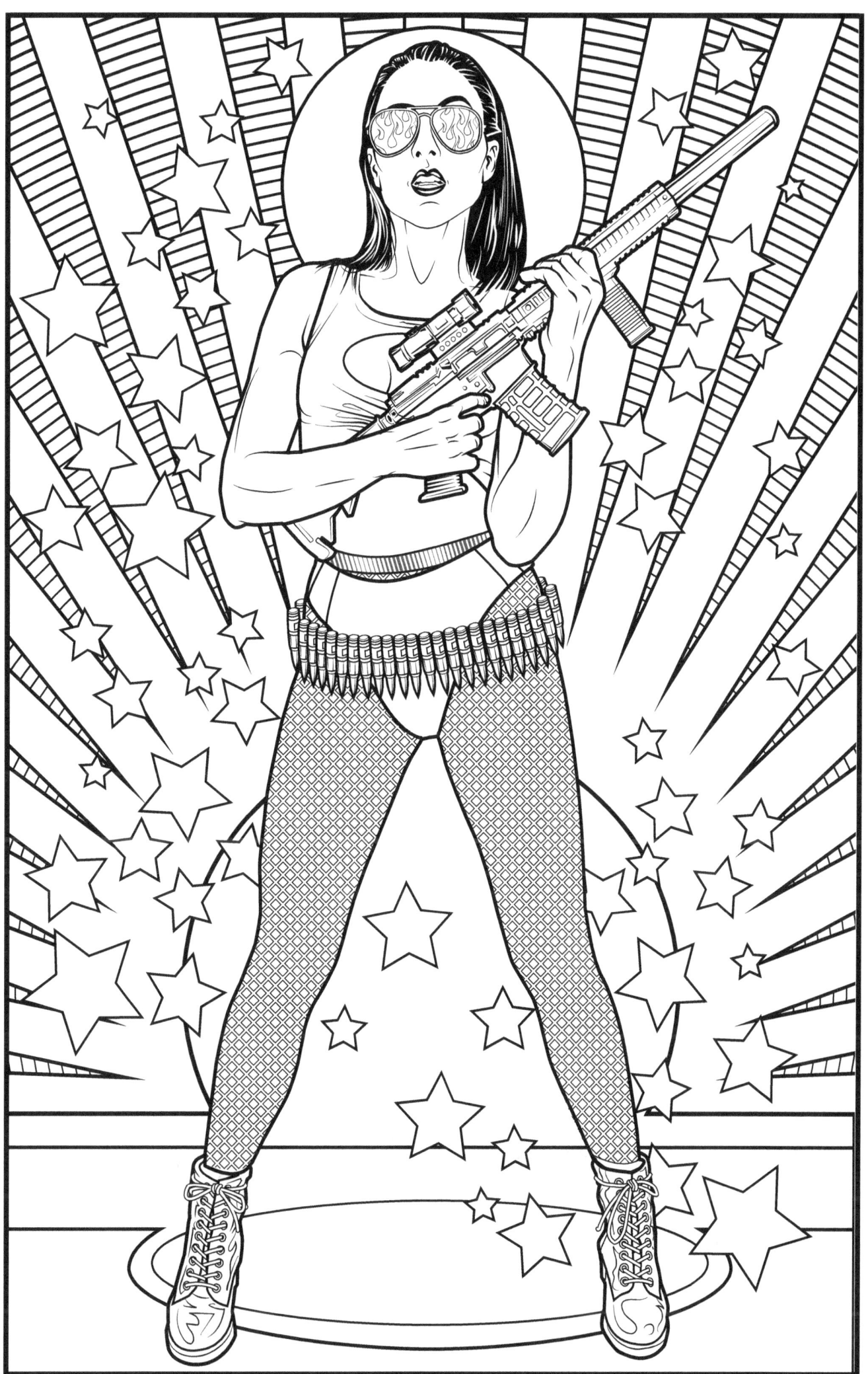

The Cyclone Of Burlesque

Model: RedBone

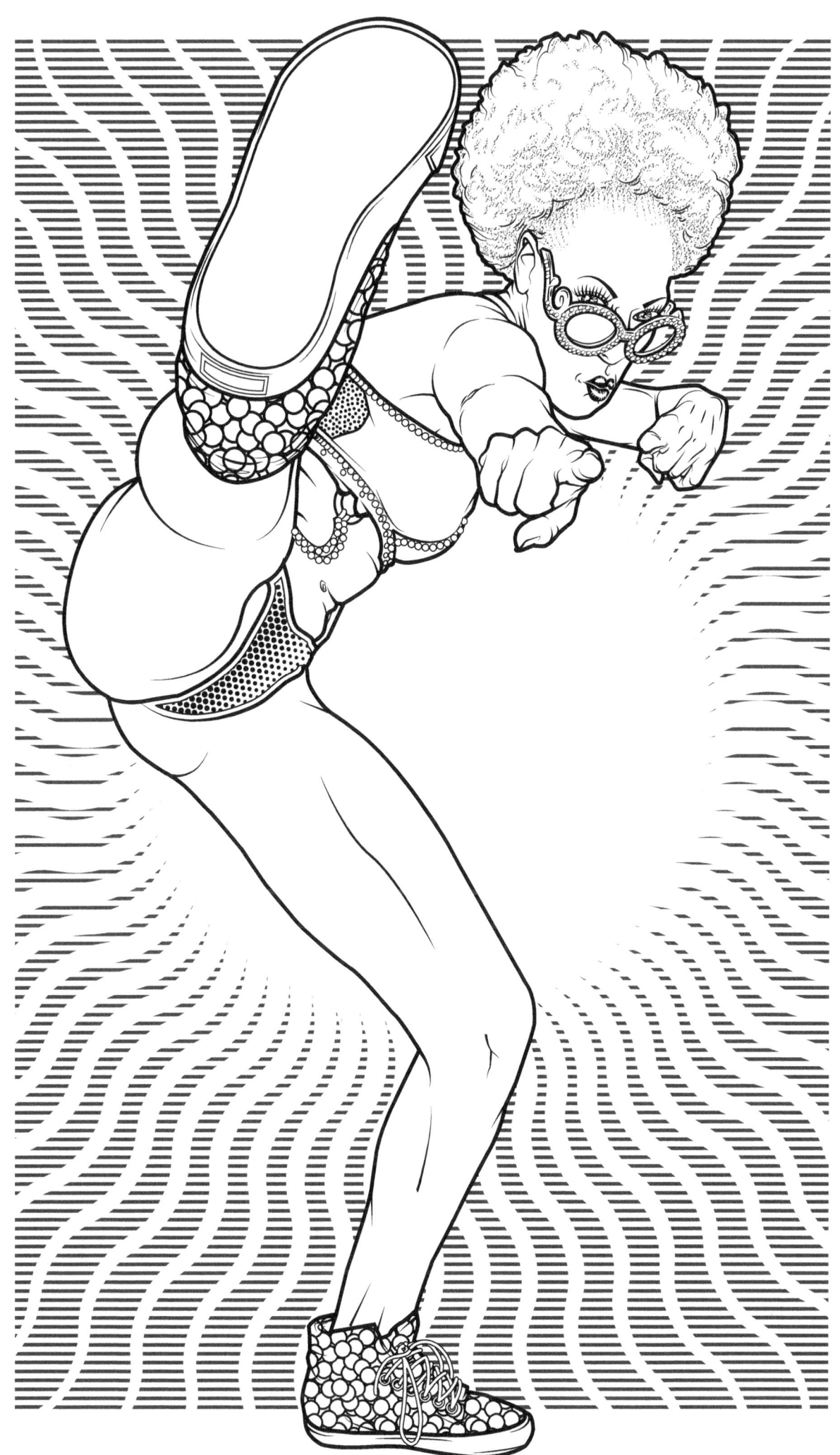

Can't Sleep? Try our Magic Apples!

Model: Rizzo Rogue

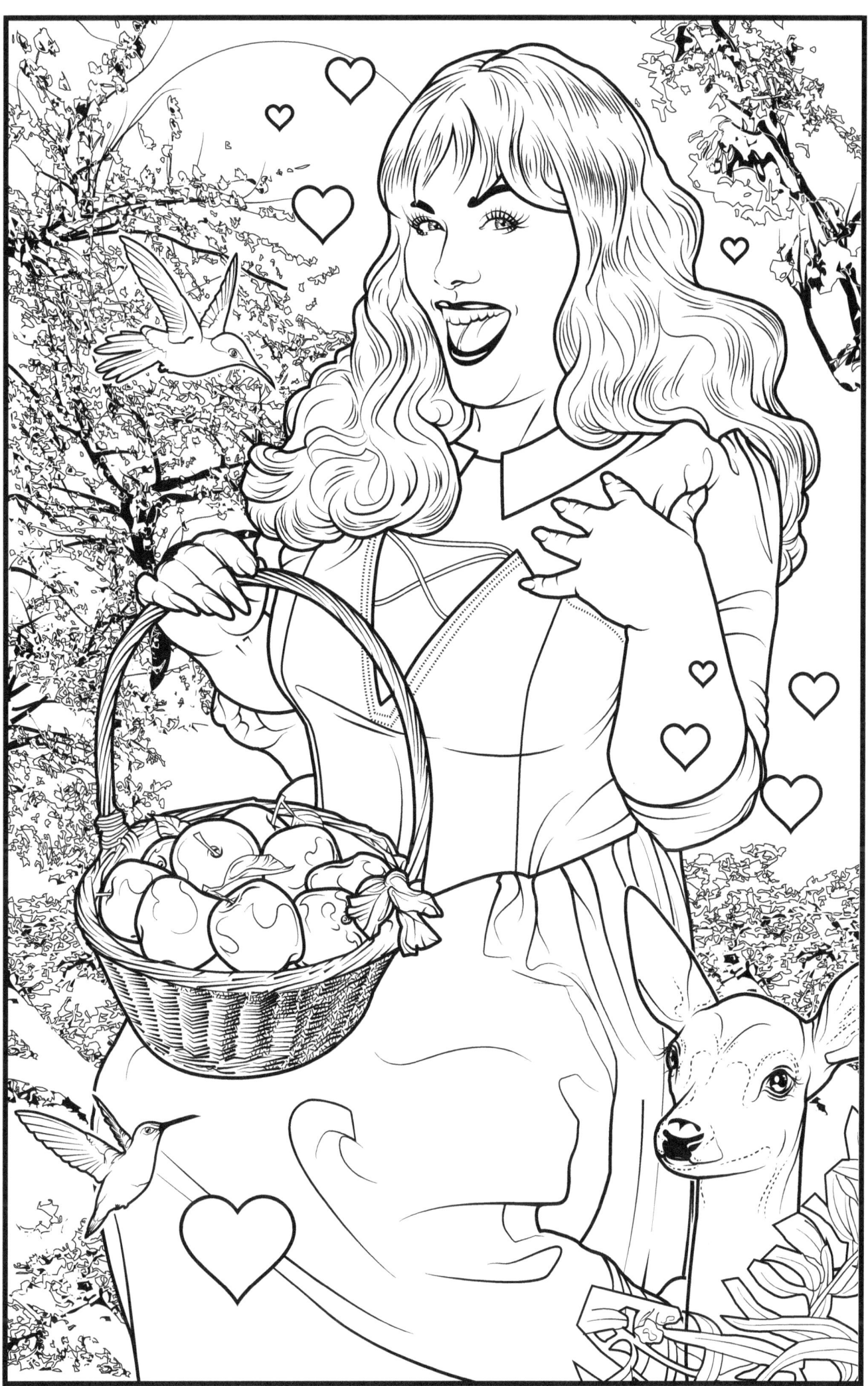

Hail To The King

Model: Seanmichael Polaris

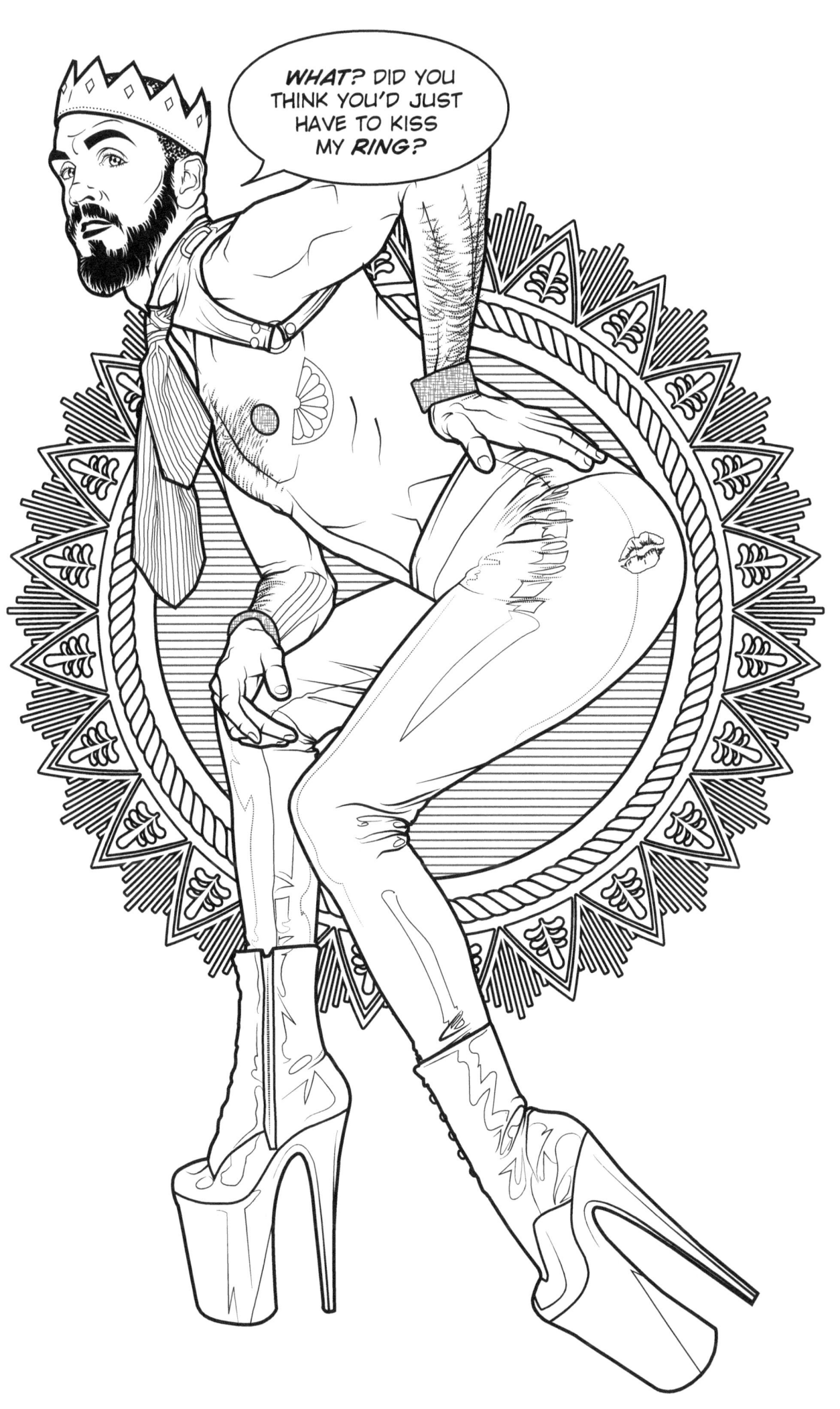

Serena Under The Sea

Model: Serena Bandtell

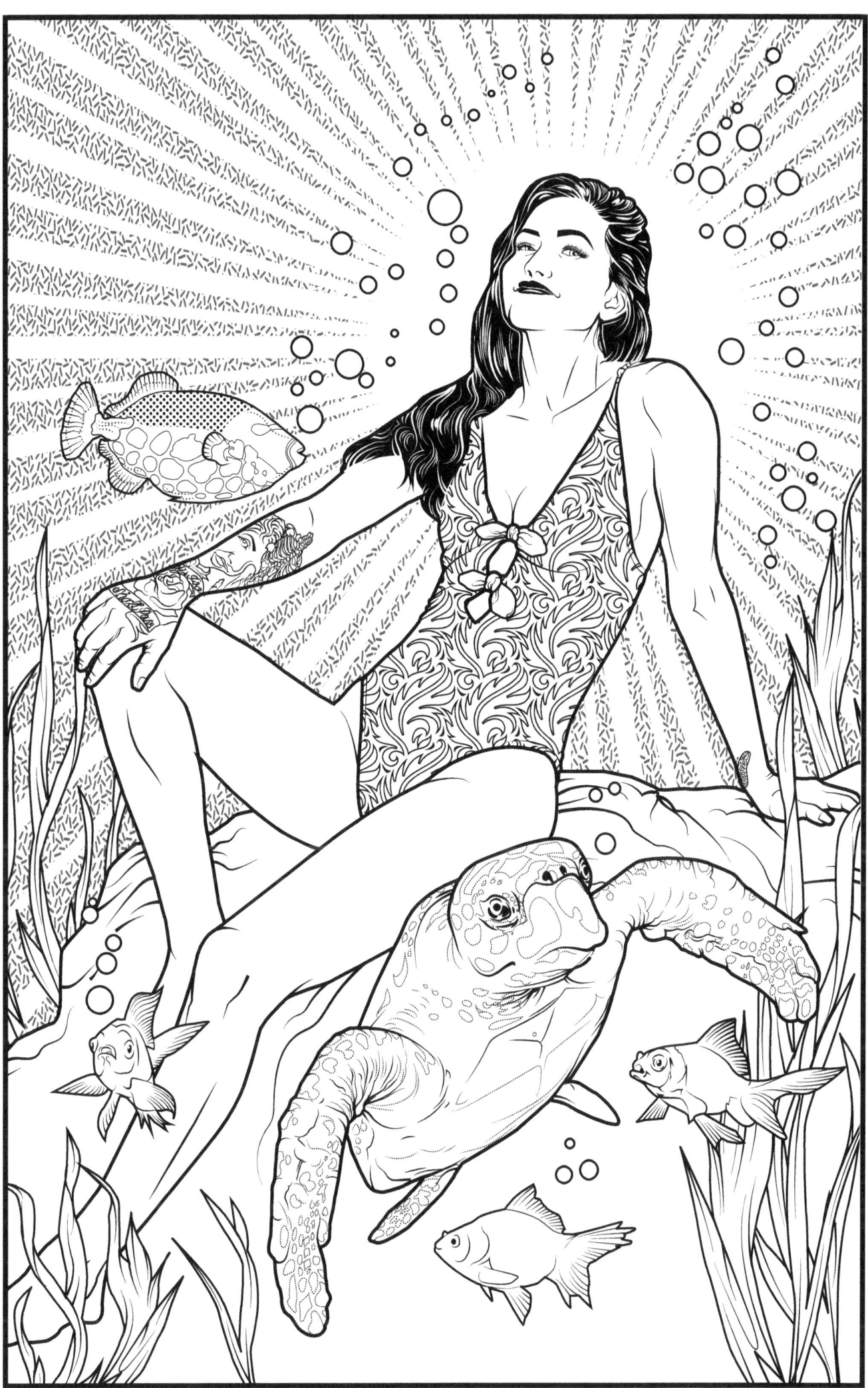

Kobayashi Maru

Model: Tease Blossom

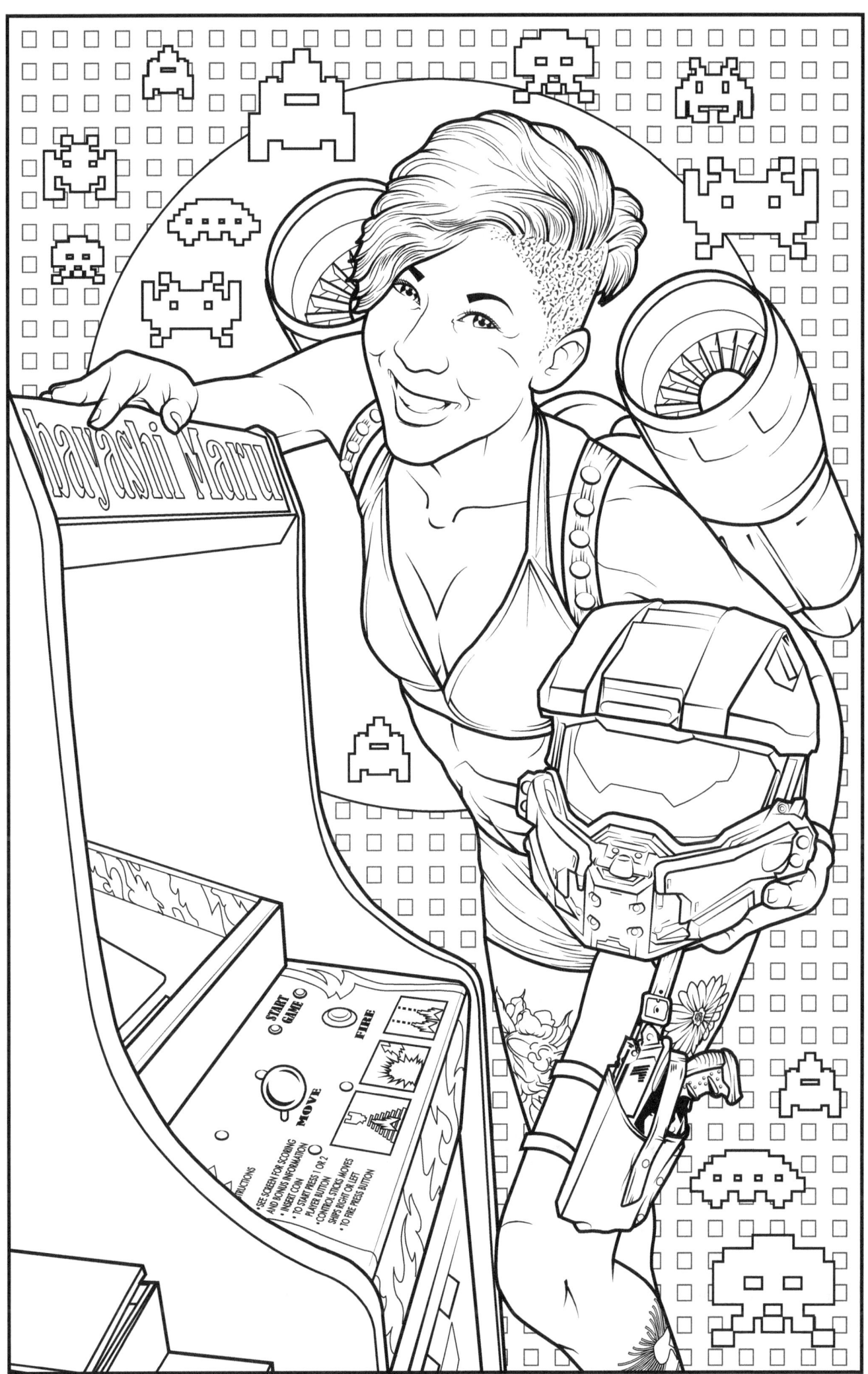

The Three Fates

Models: Dem Foxie Femmes:

Pixie Vanílle, Frankie Fictitious and Sweet Belize

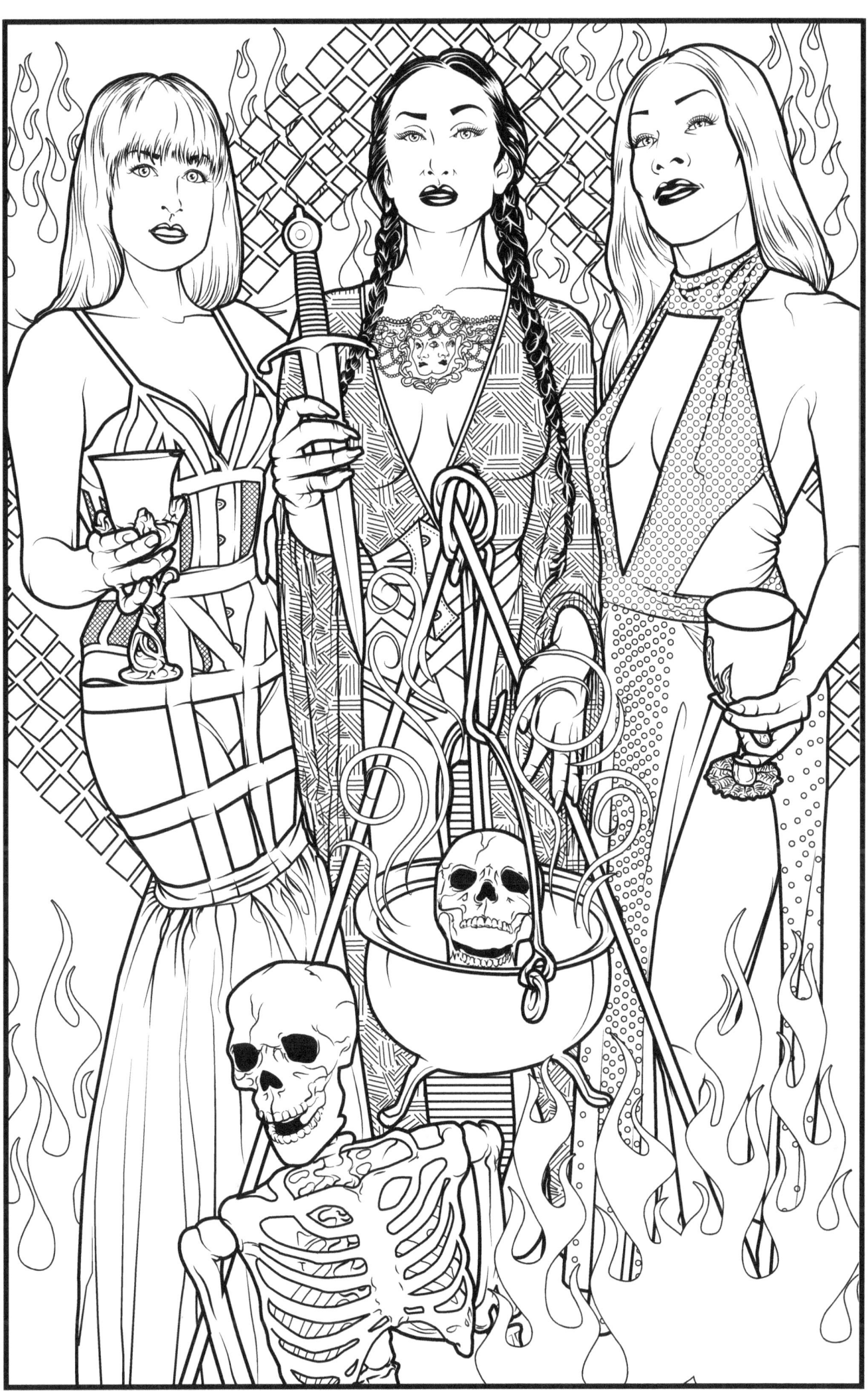

The Show Goes On

Model: Vixi Vale

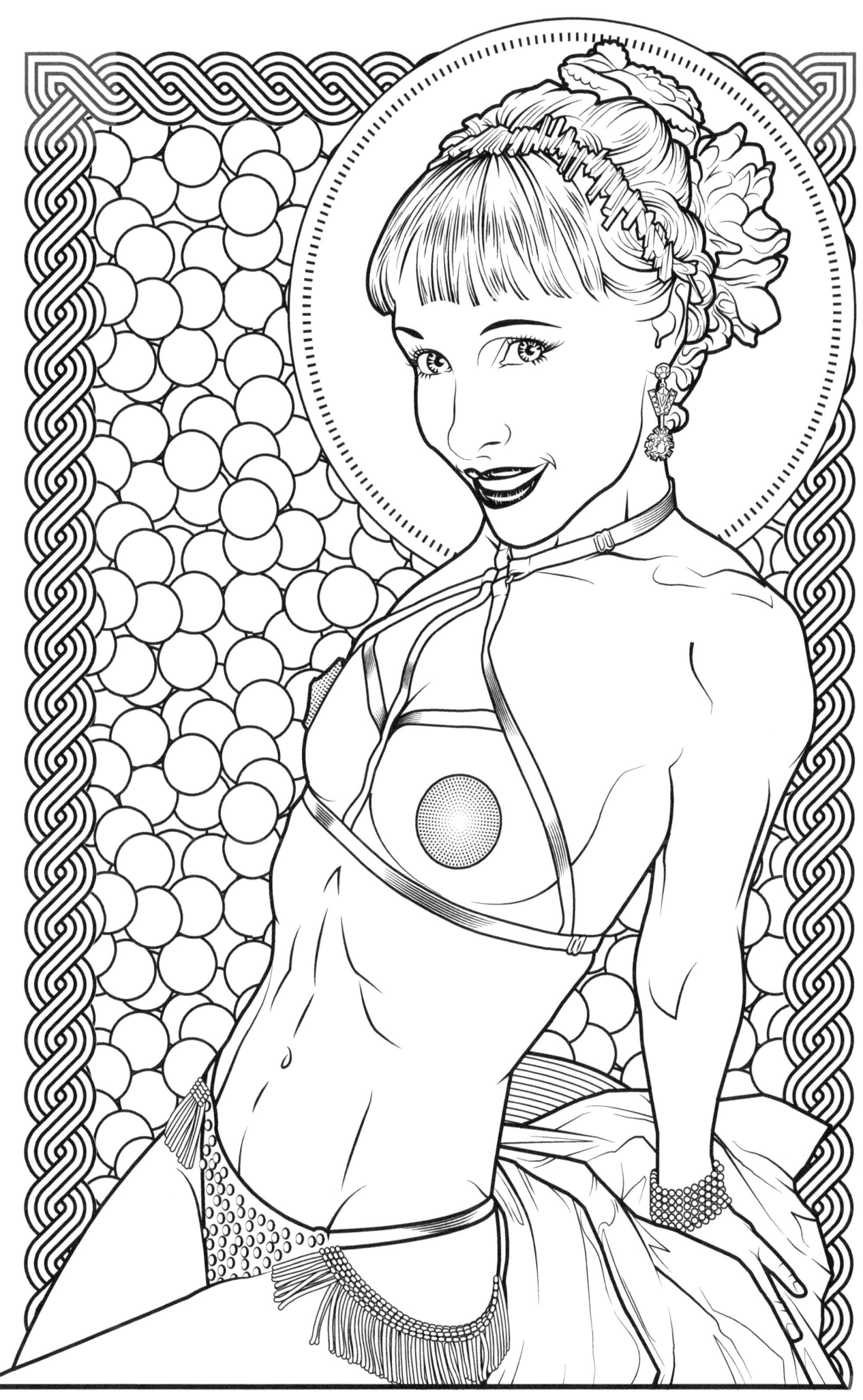

Want To Play A Game?

Model: Ellie Kimiko

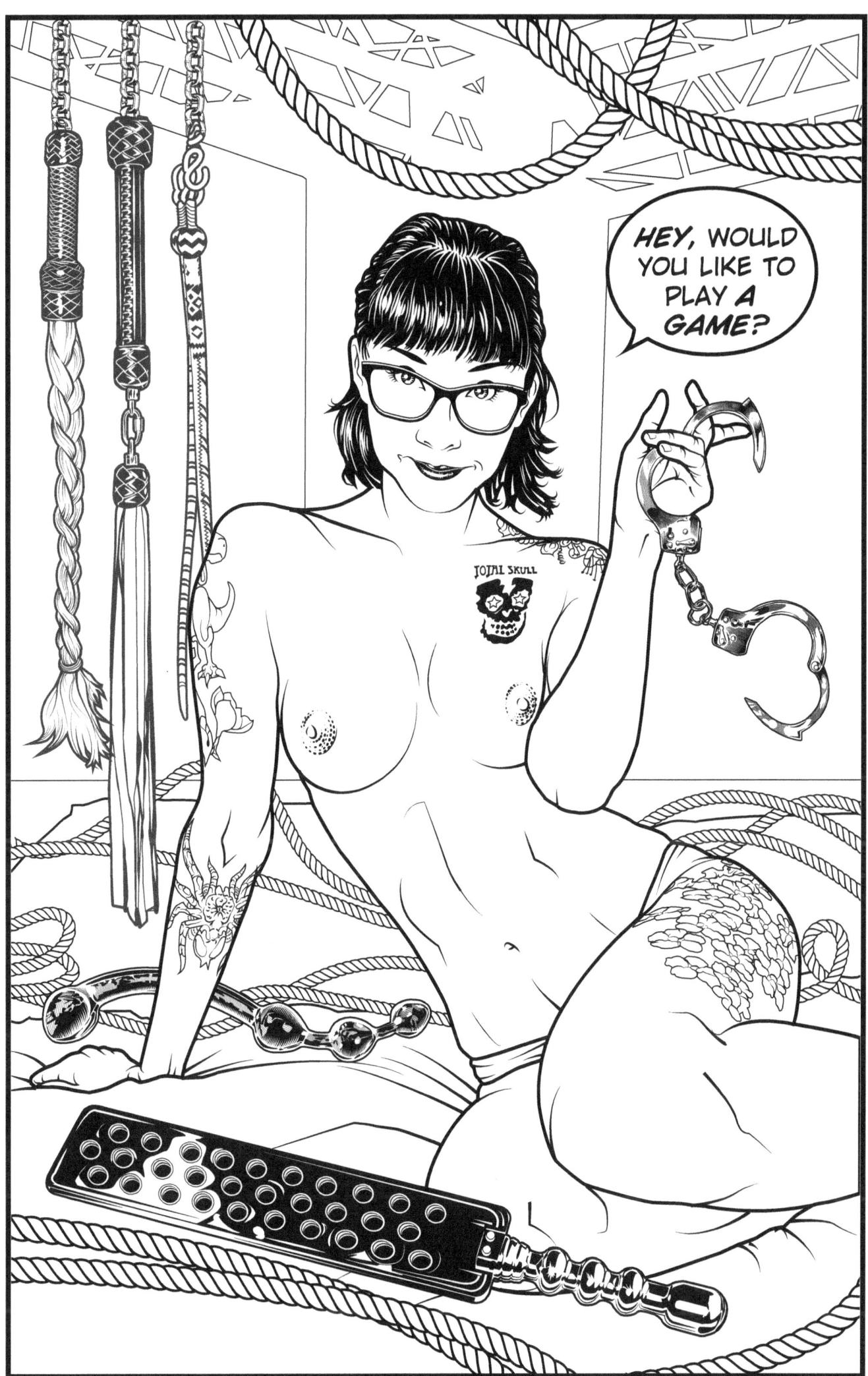

Cold Hard Stare

Model: Kory Vixen

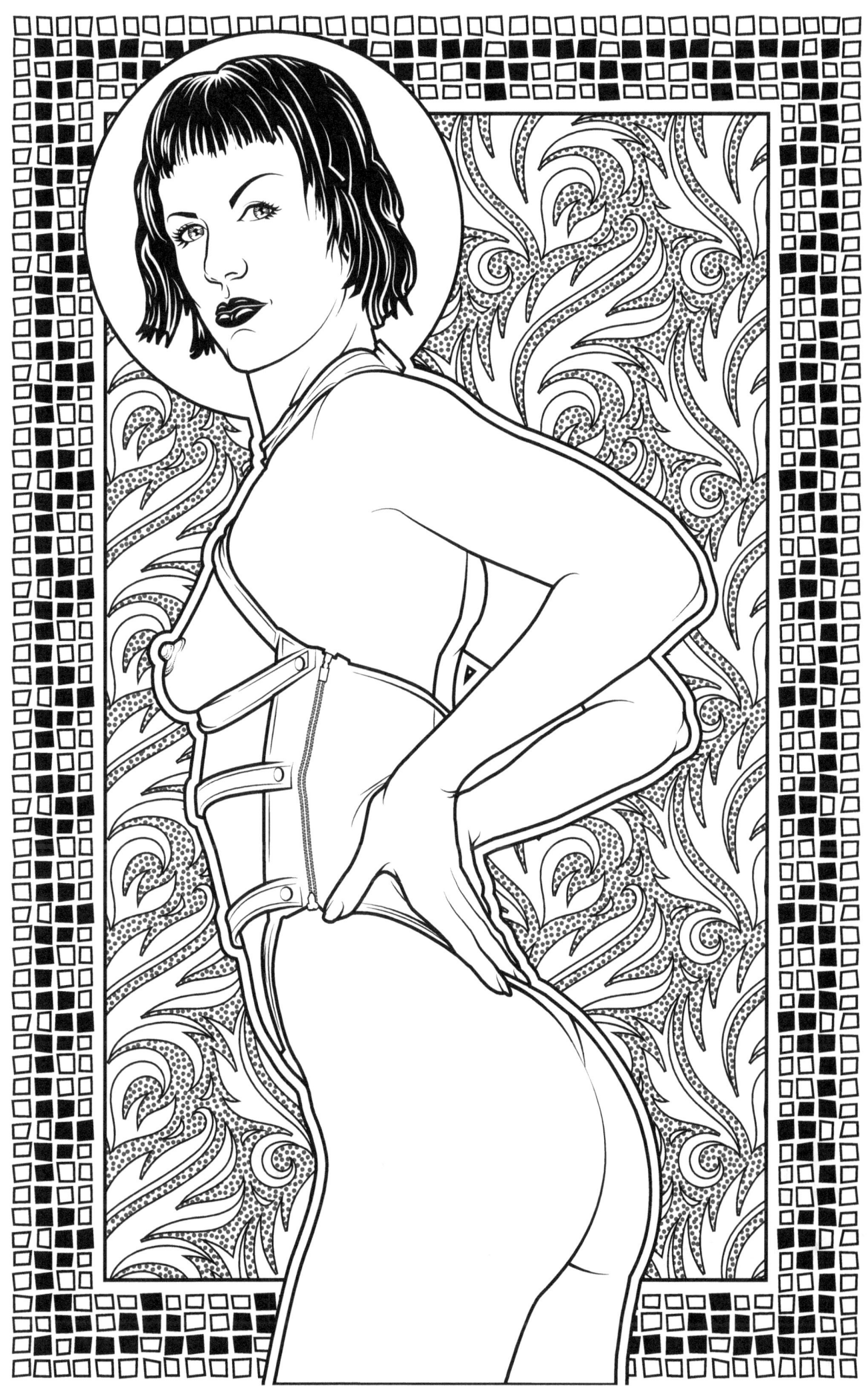

Rhythm Section

Model: Calvaleigh Rasmussen

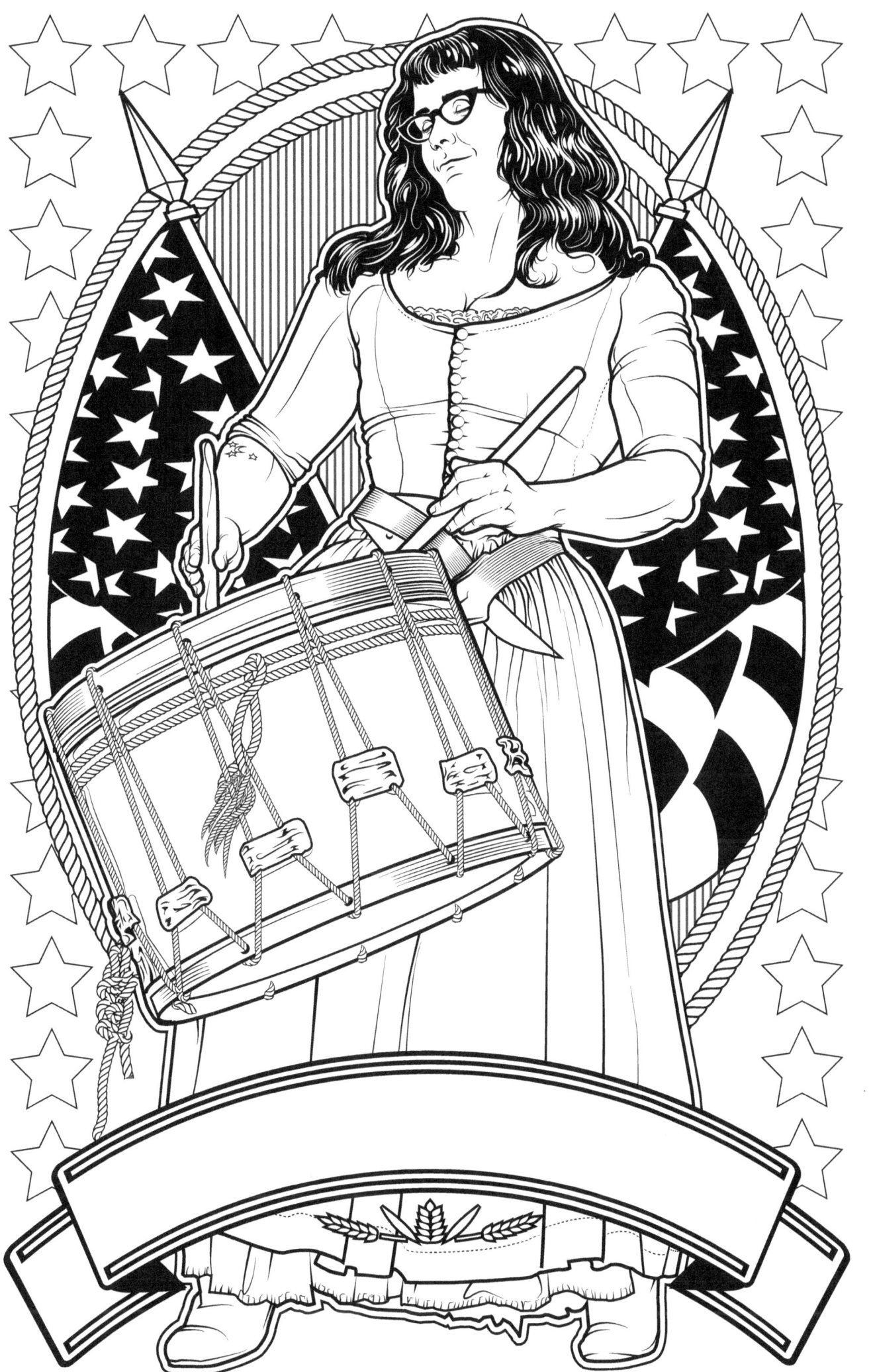

We Are Starstuff

Model: Qu'in De La Noche

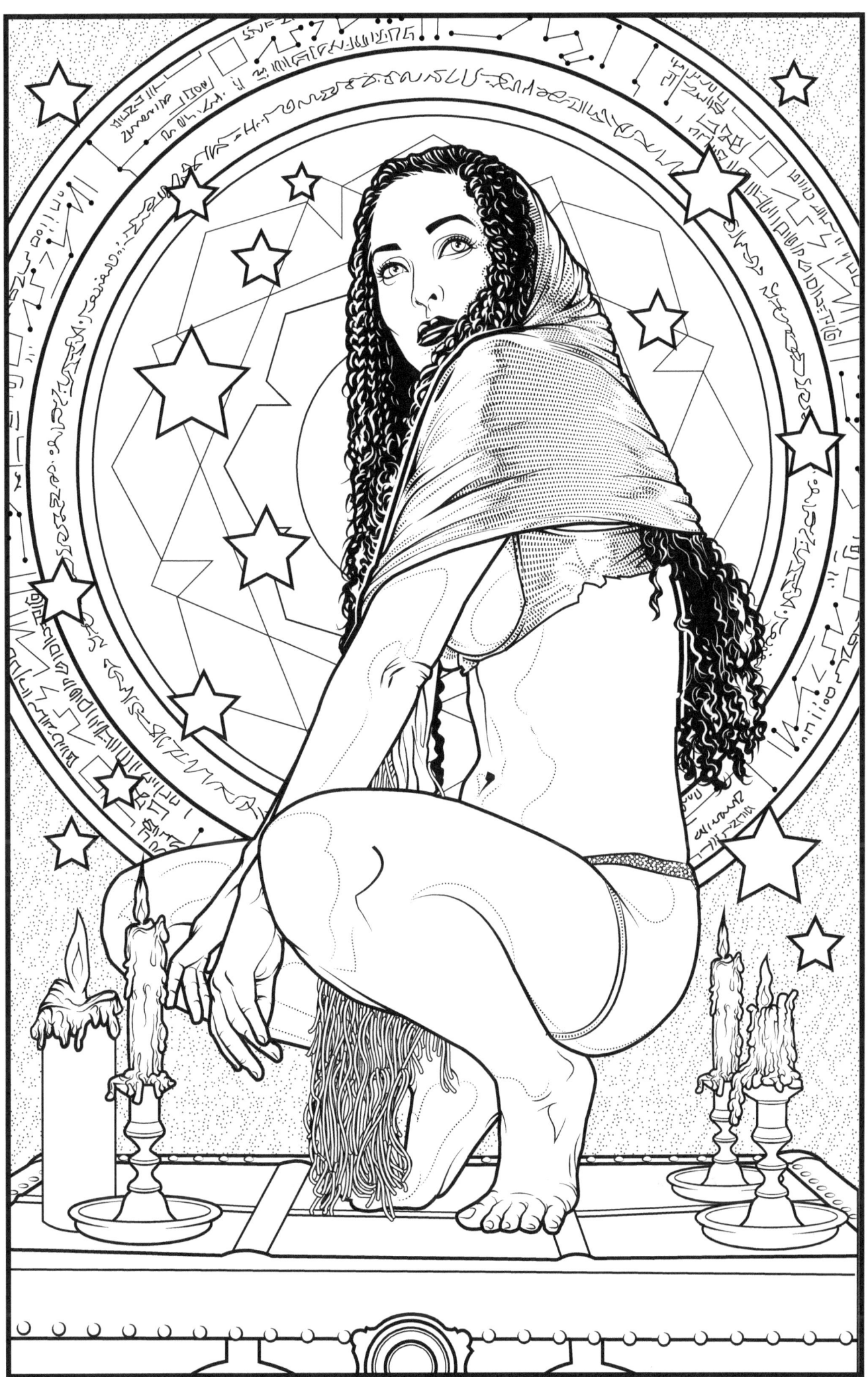

Game Changer

Model: Ophelia Coeur de Noir

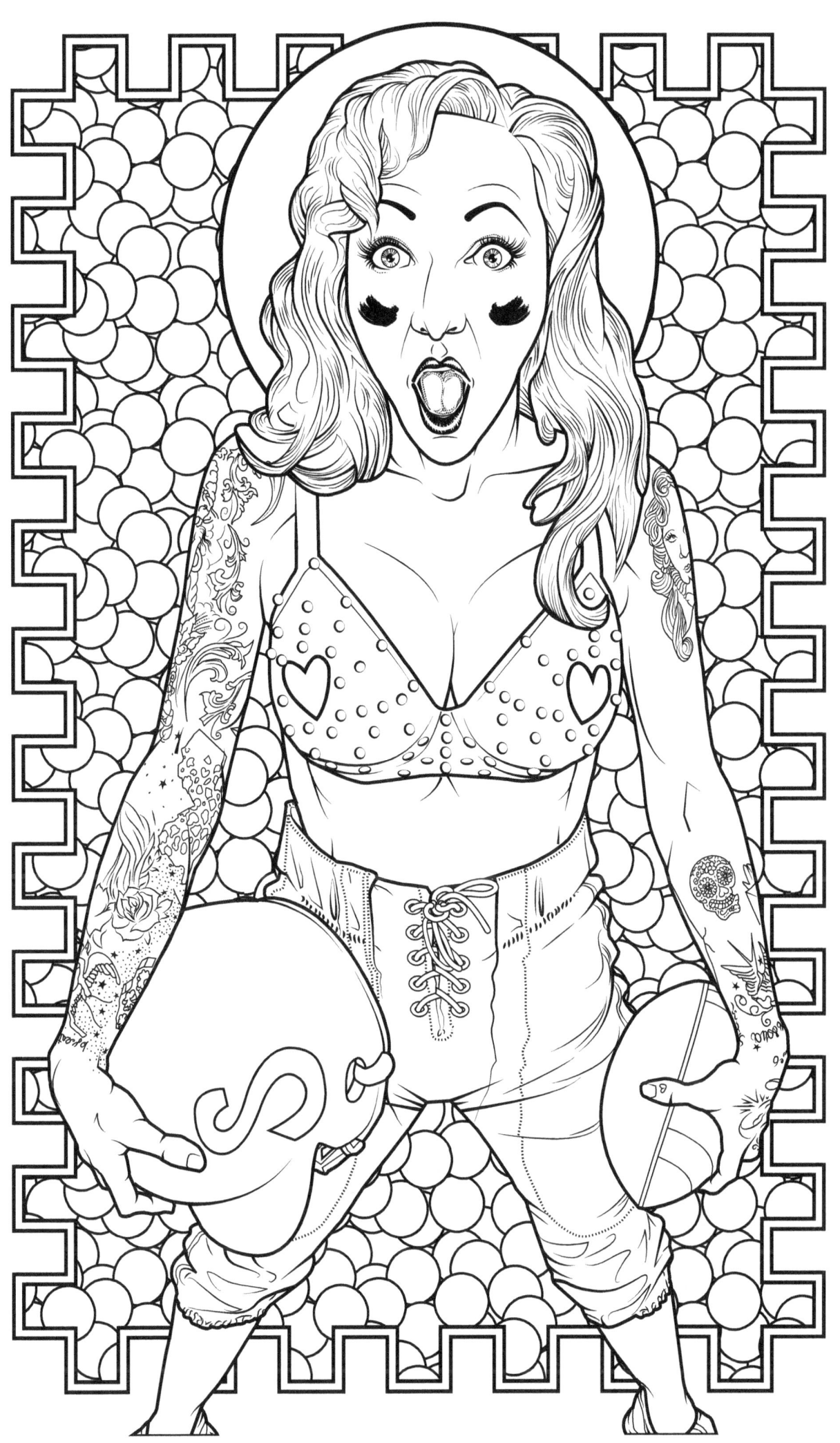

Ready To Play

Model: Dani_Red

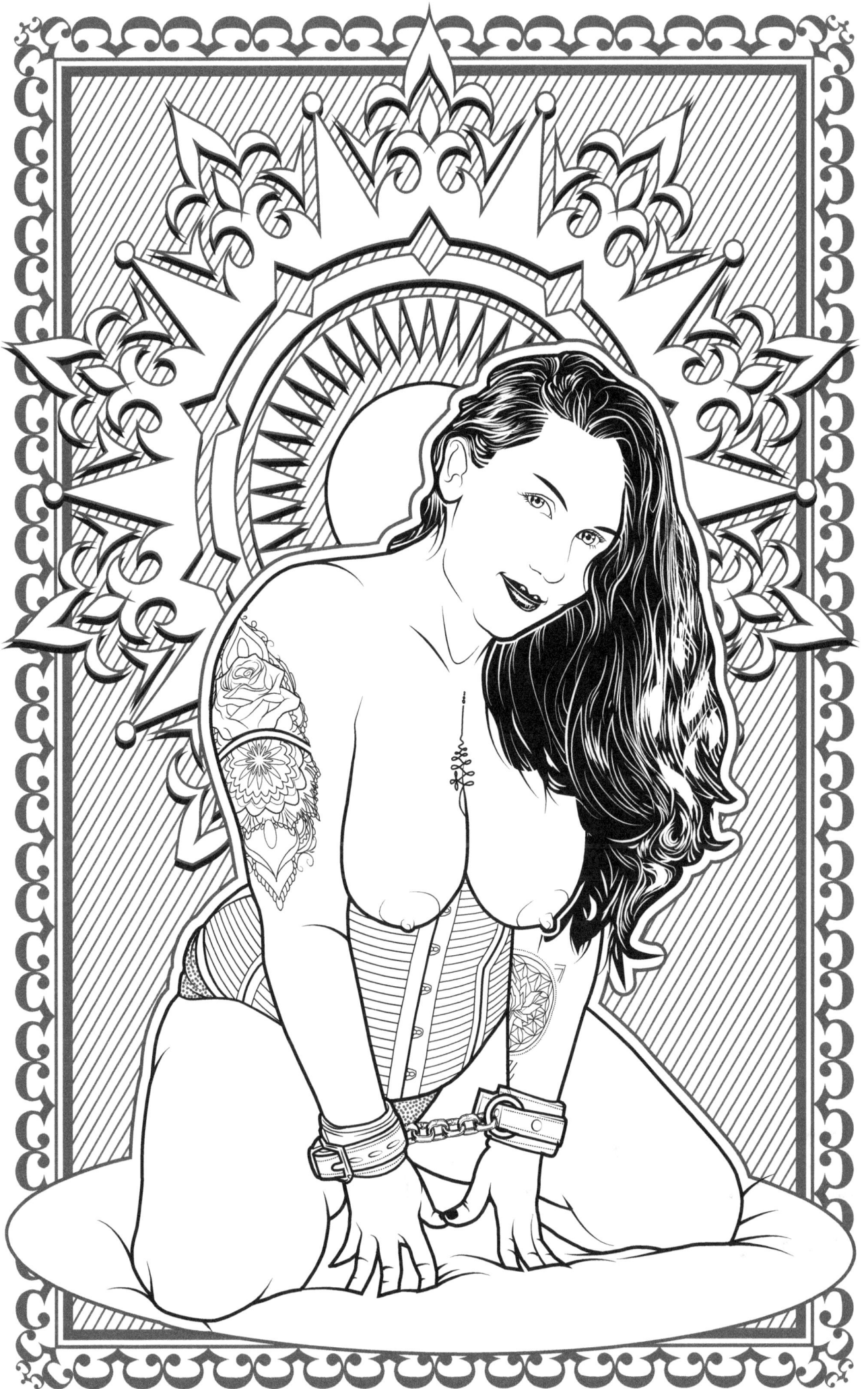

Good Morning

Model: Zille Defue

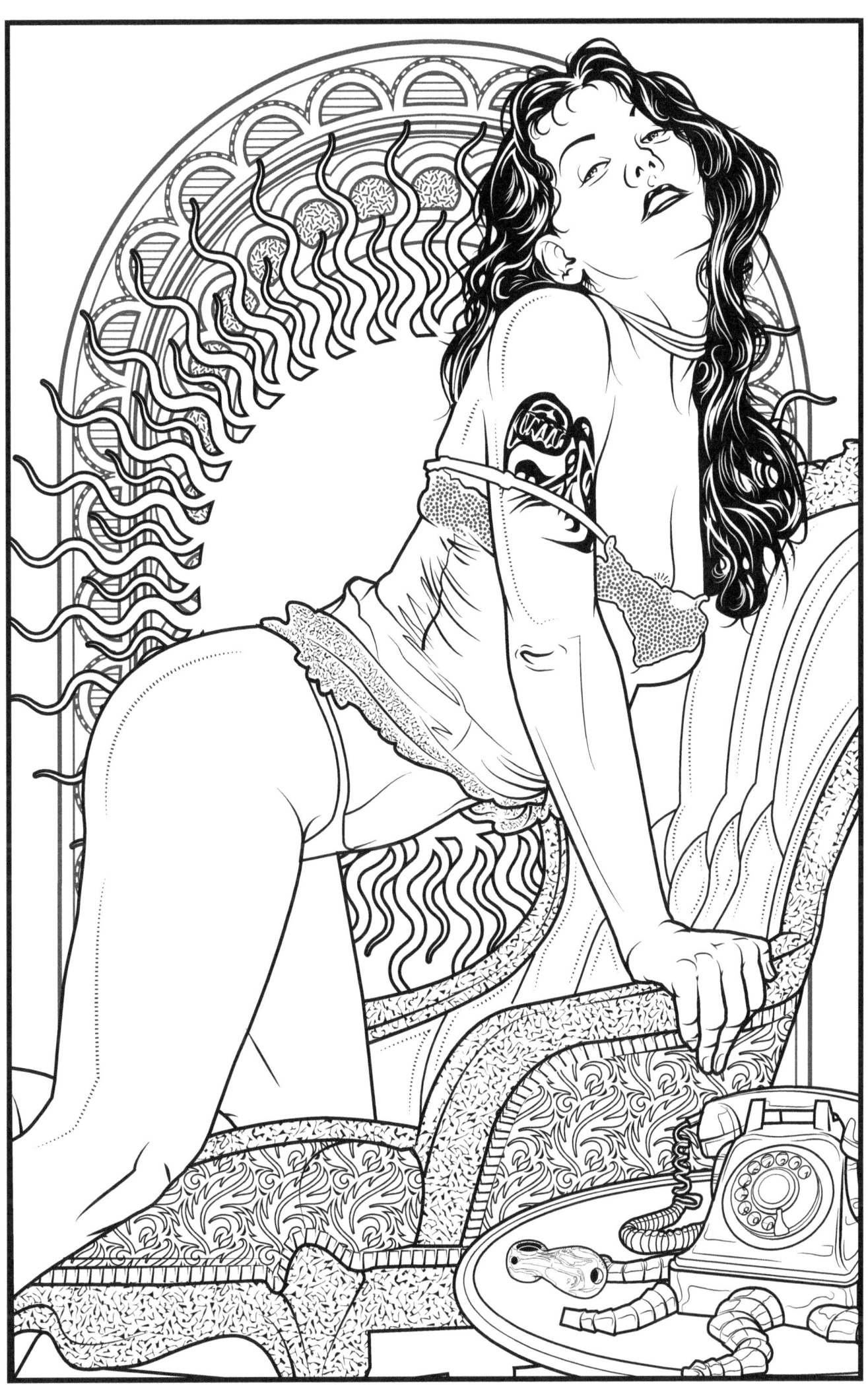

Rockin' Rasa

Model: Rasa Vitalia

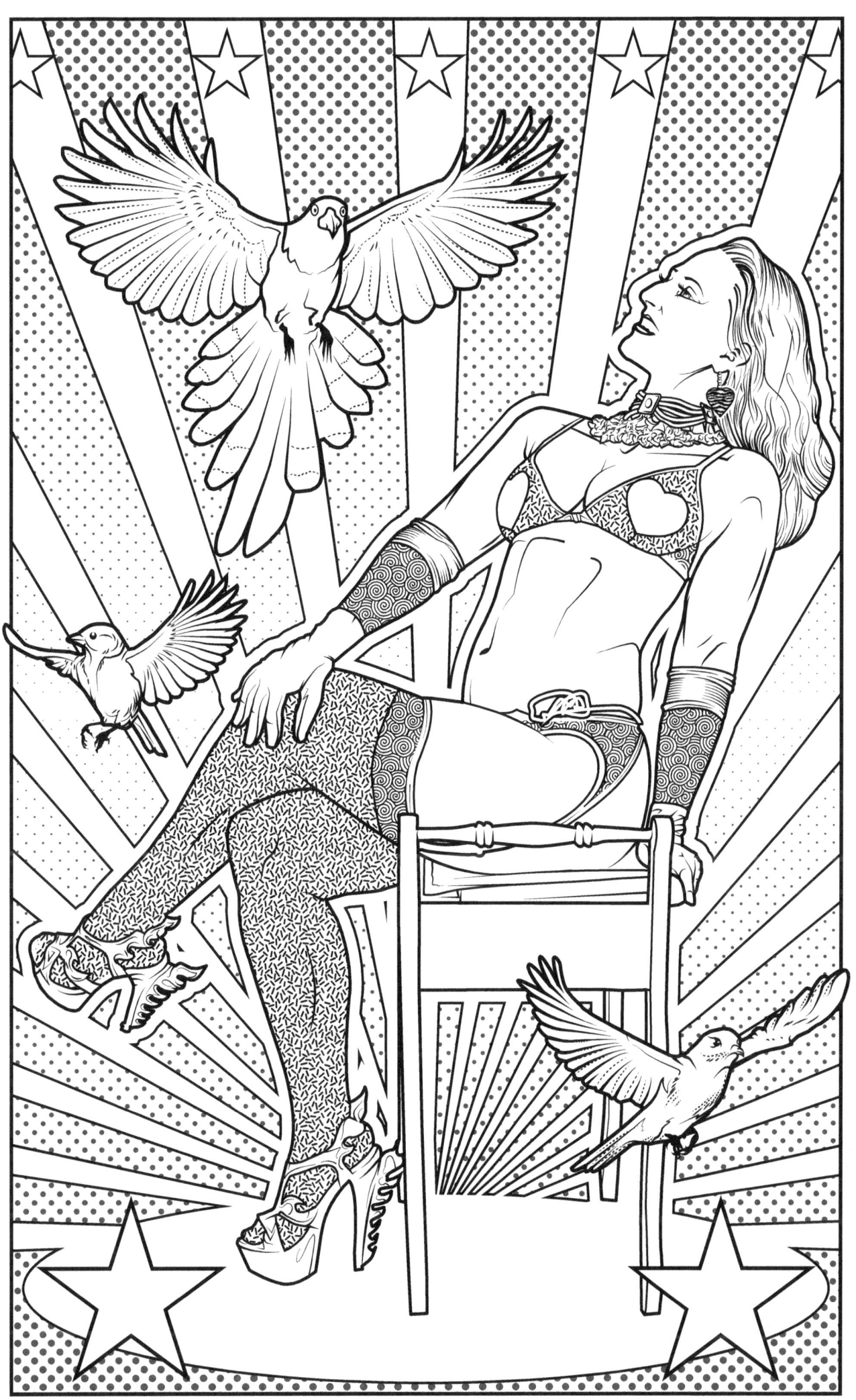

Bad Wolf

Model: Major Suttle-Tease

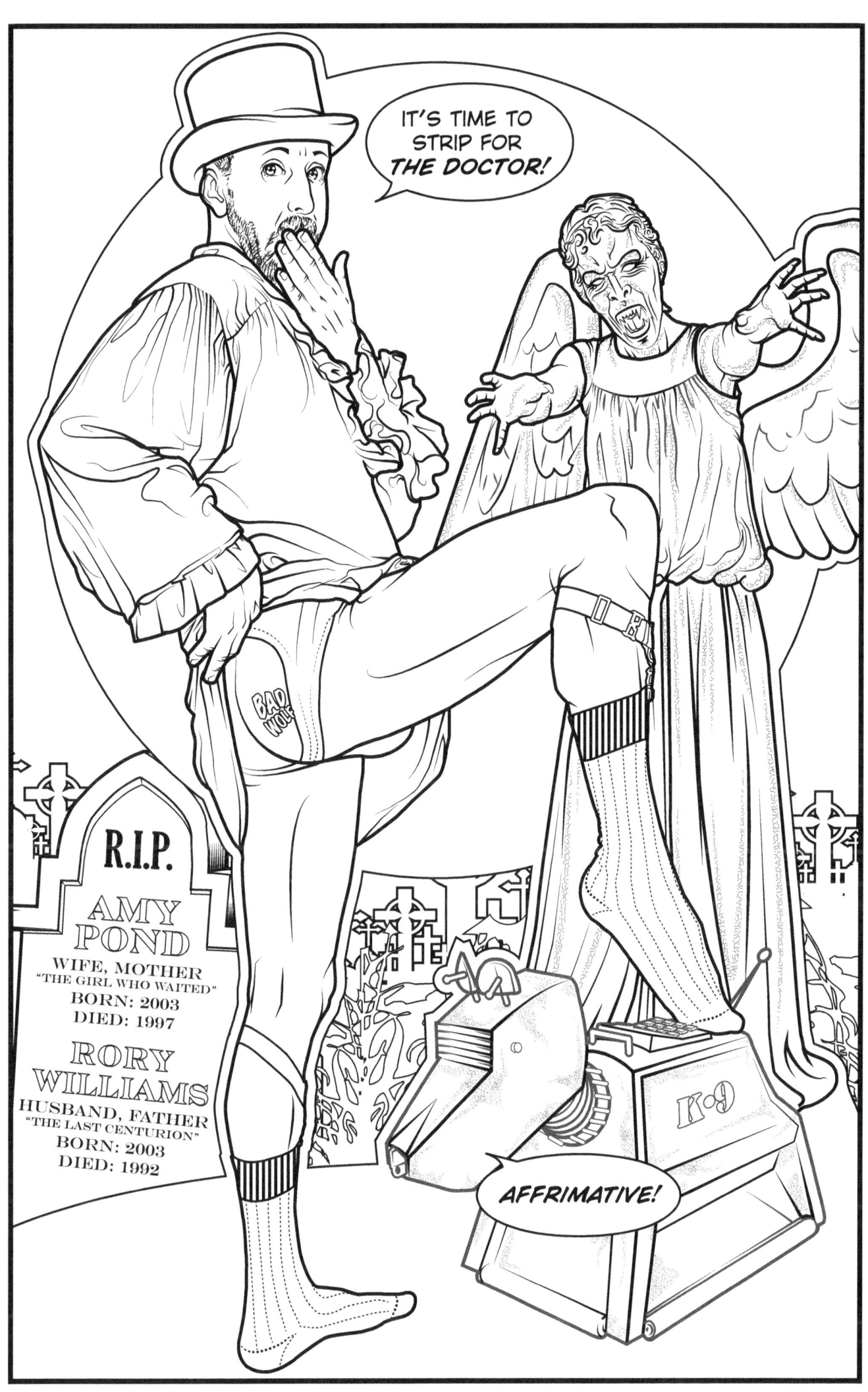

Plague Mask

Model: Kitty Meow

Plague Mask Designer: Mercy Daae Studio

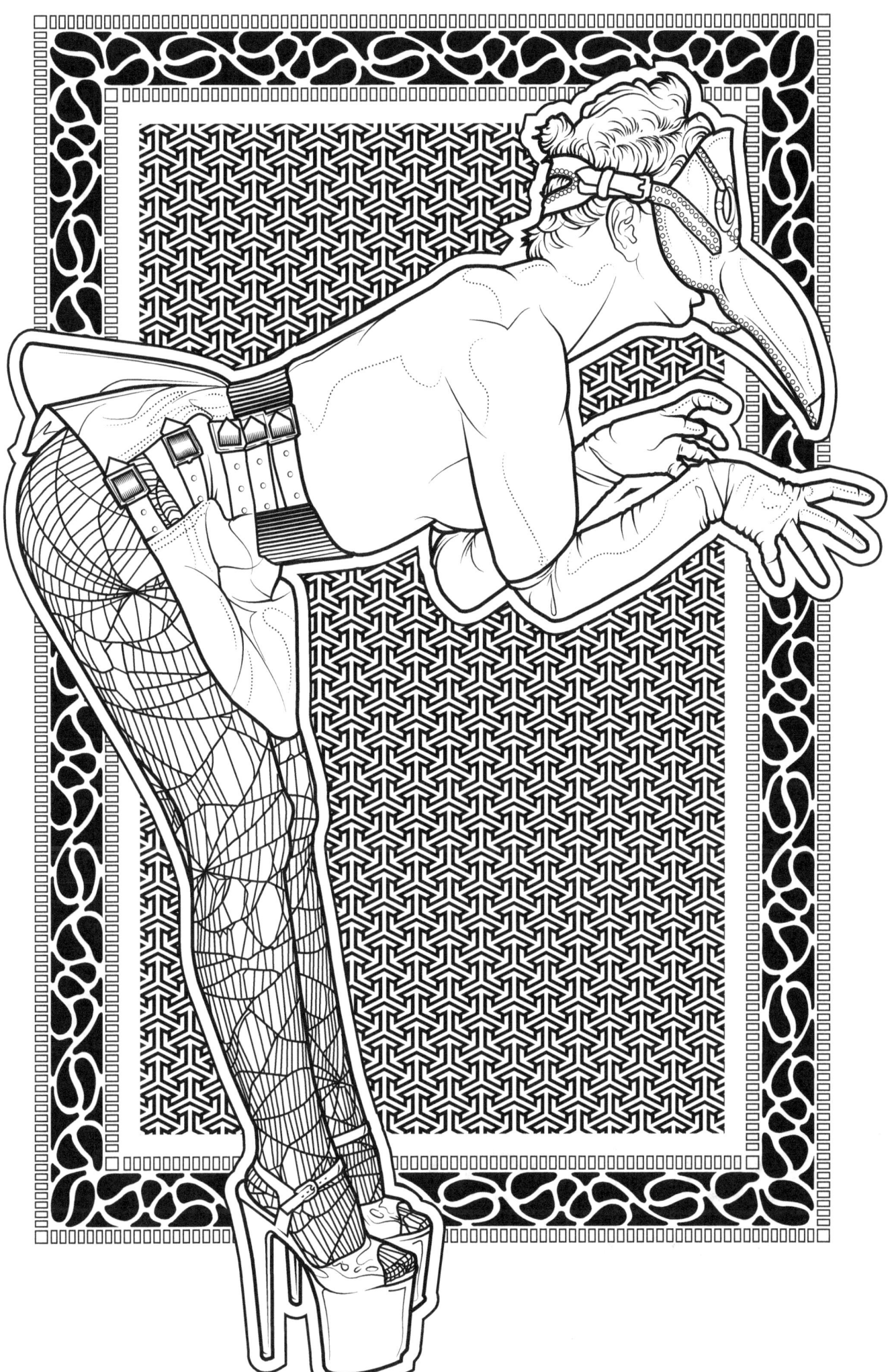

Troop Leader

Model: Adriana Roberts from BOOTIESF!

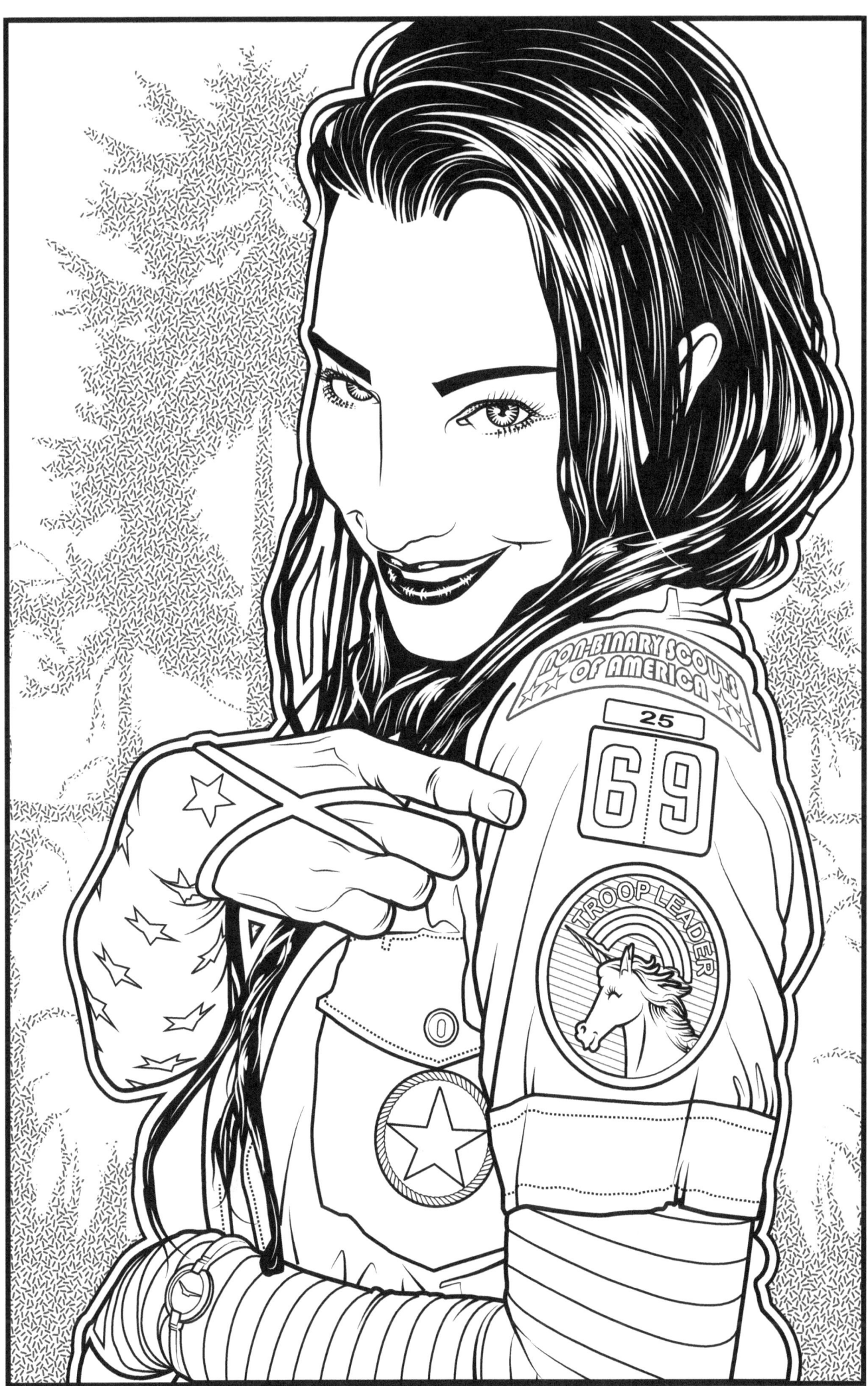

The Lady Is A Vamp

Model: Trixxie Carr

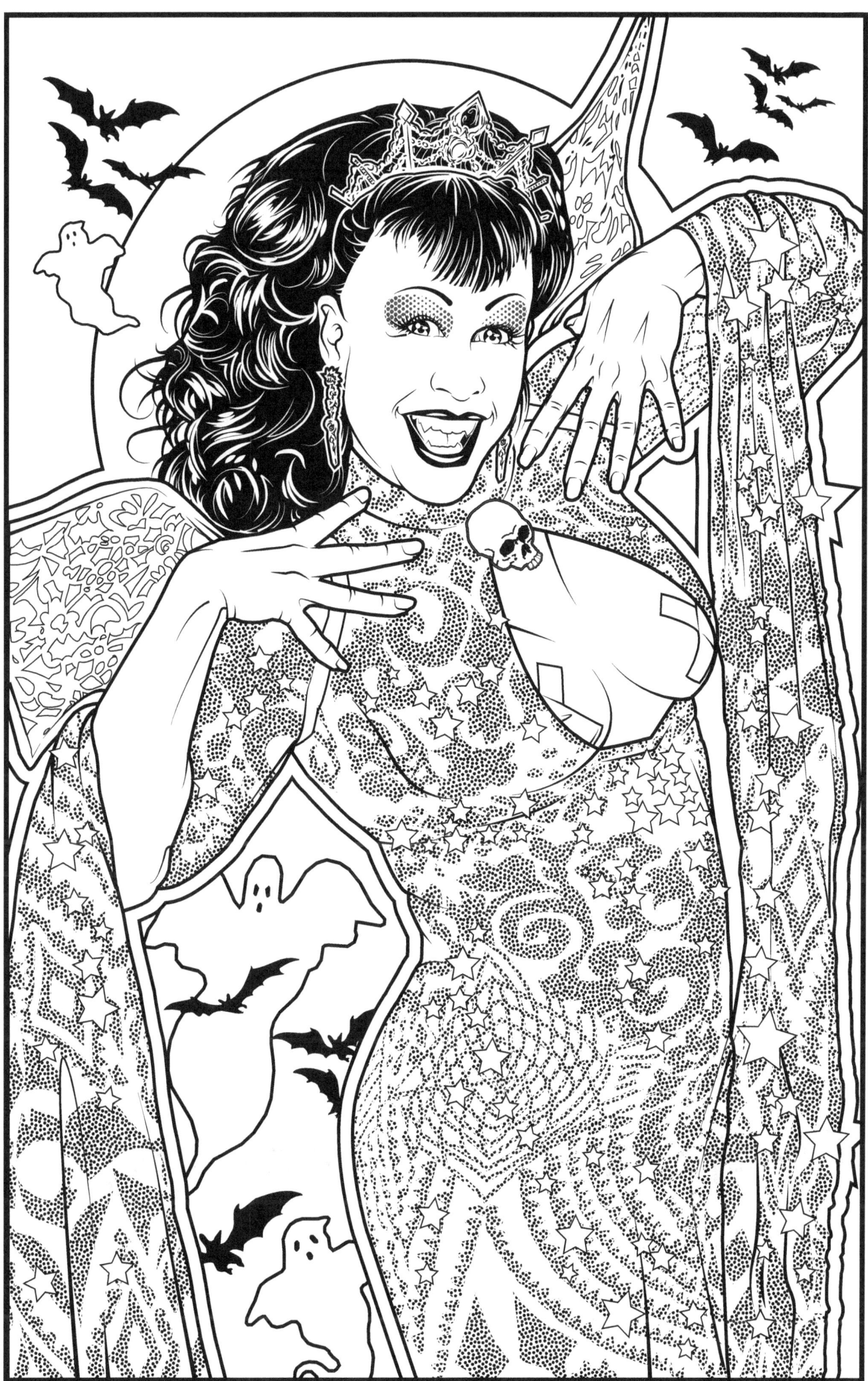

Tree of Knowledge

Model: Libby Loo

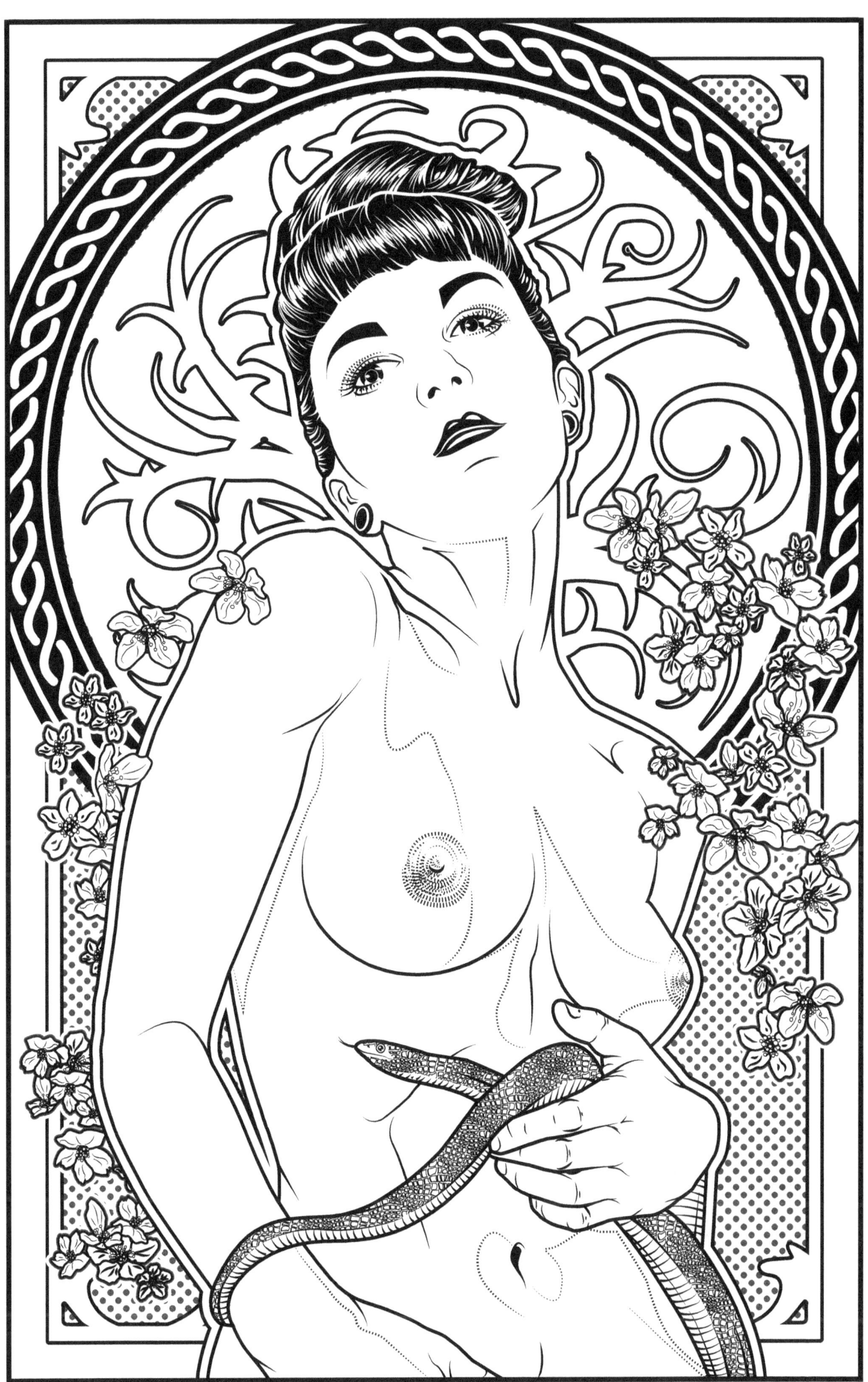

Cooling Off

Model: __nonnie_97

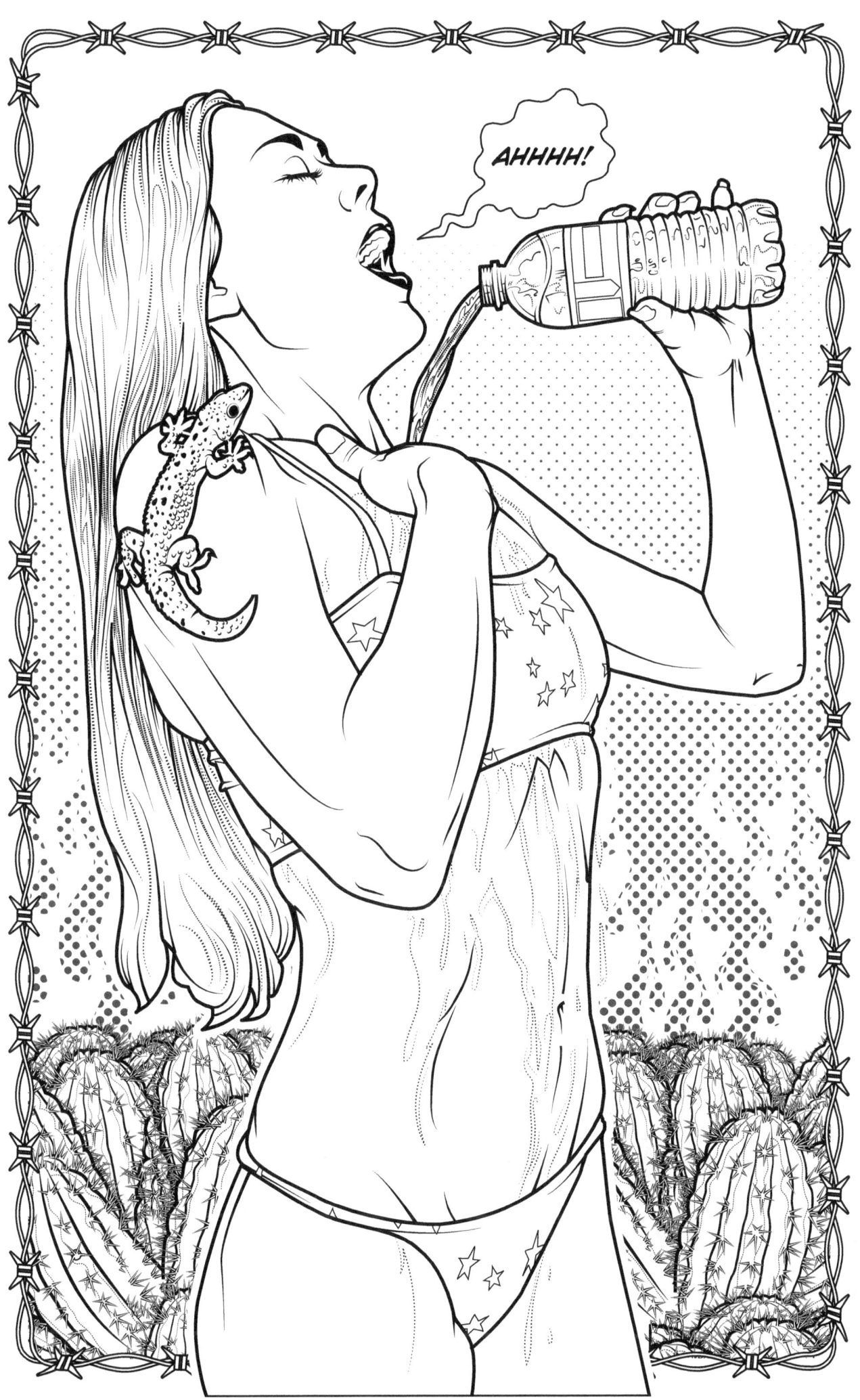

Friendly Neighborhood Pansexual Sparkly Cat Lady Trash Mouth

Model: Ifn Whendy

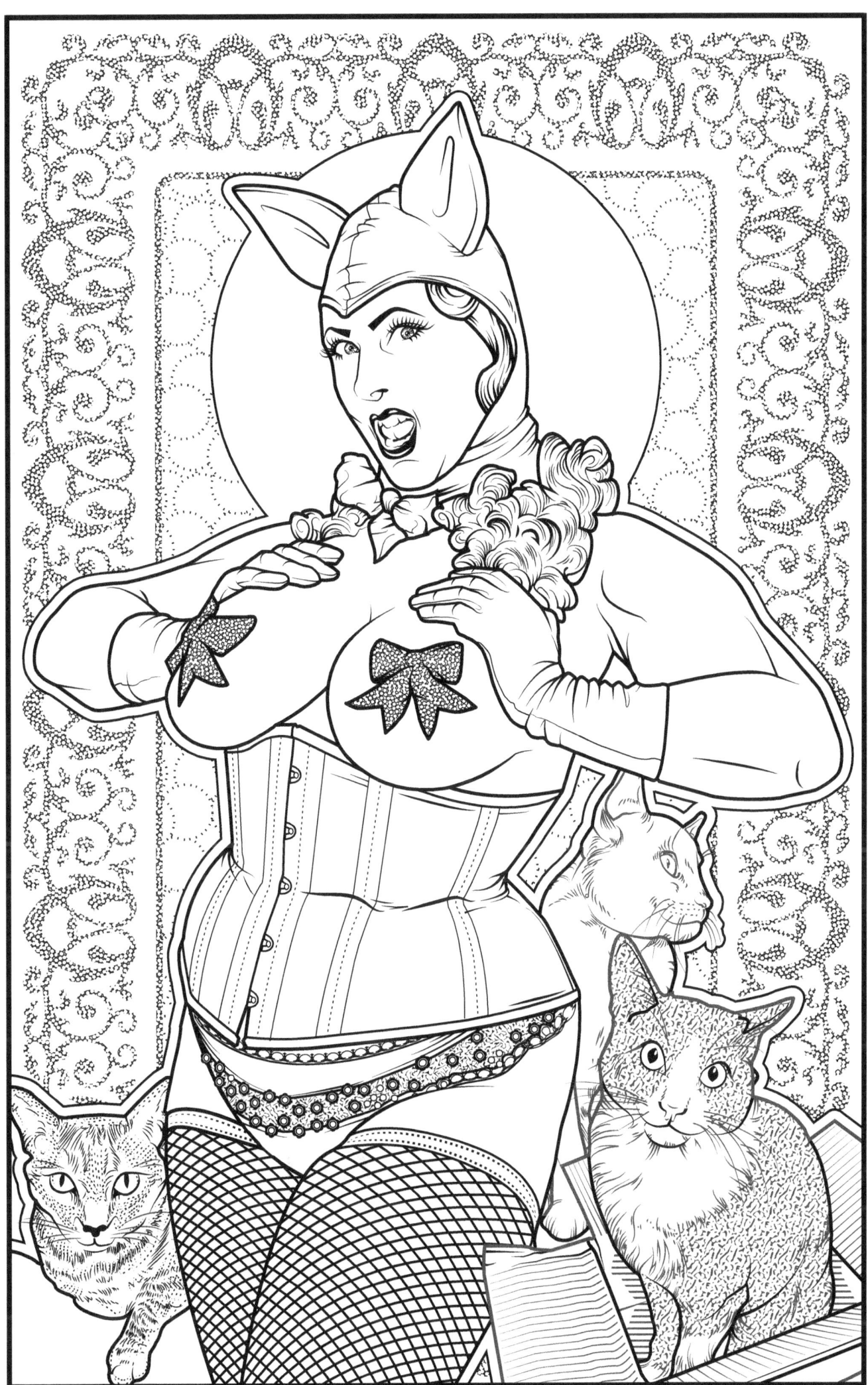

Black Arts Matter

Model: Mone't Ha-Sidi

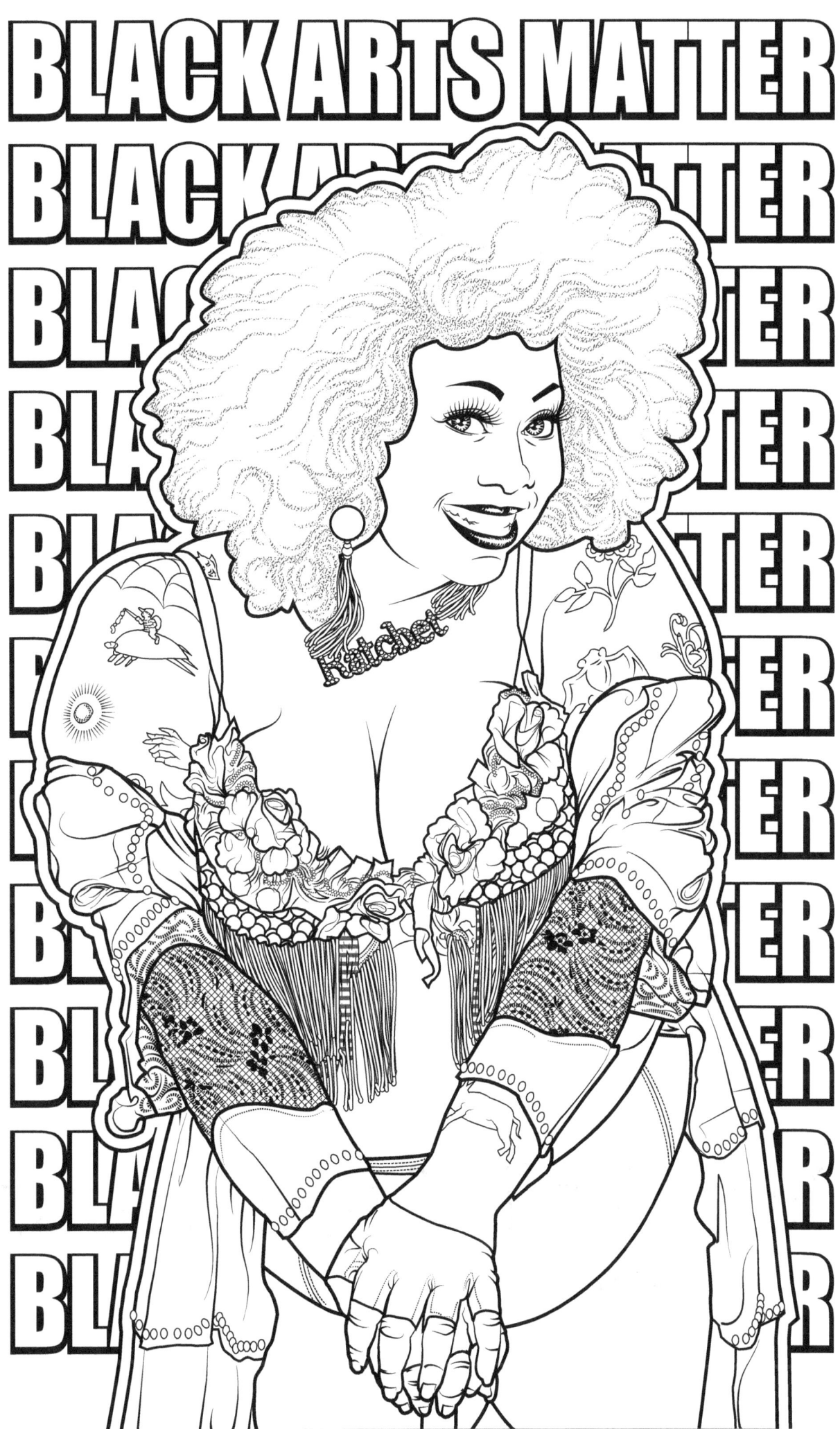

Dirty Talk After Hours

Model: Rain DeGrey

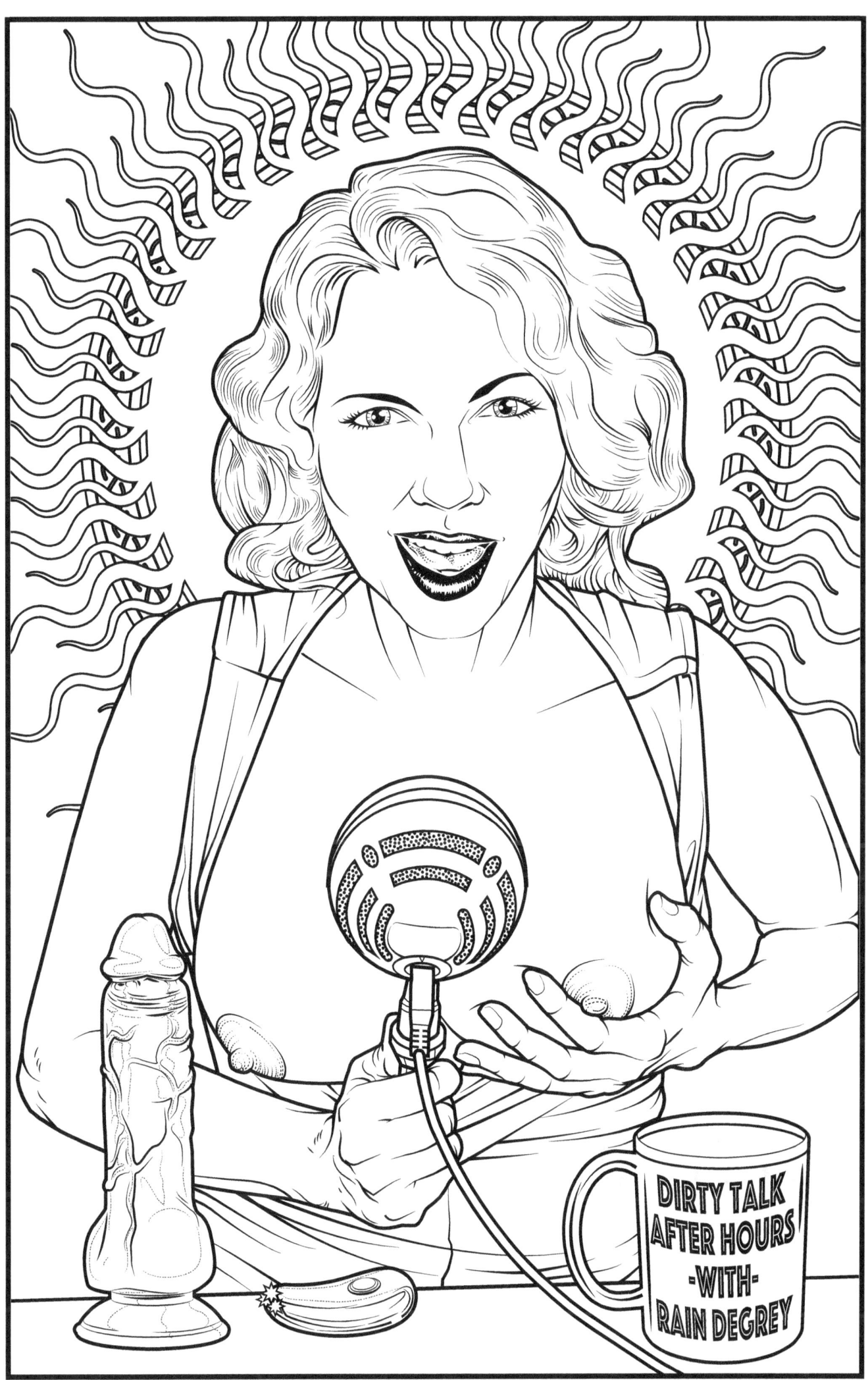

Spanking Dani

Model: Dani_Red

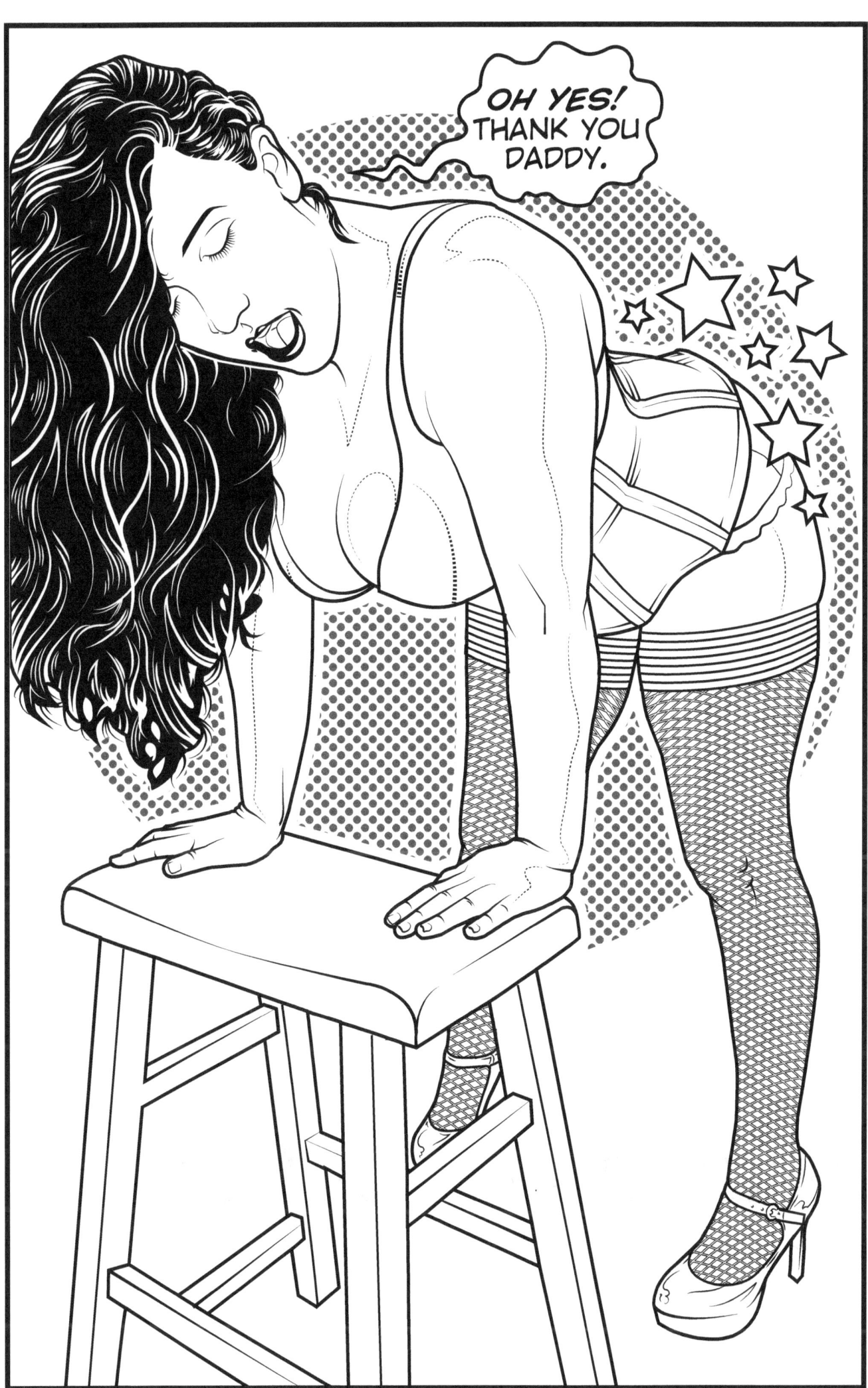

Mistress's Coffee

Model: -promethea-

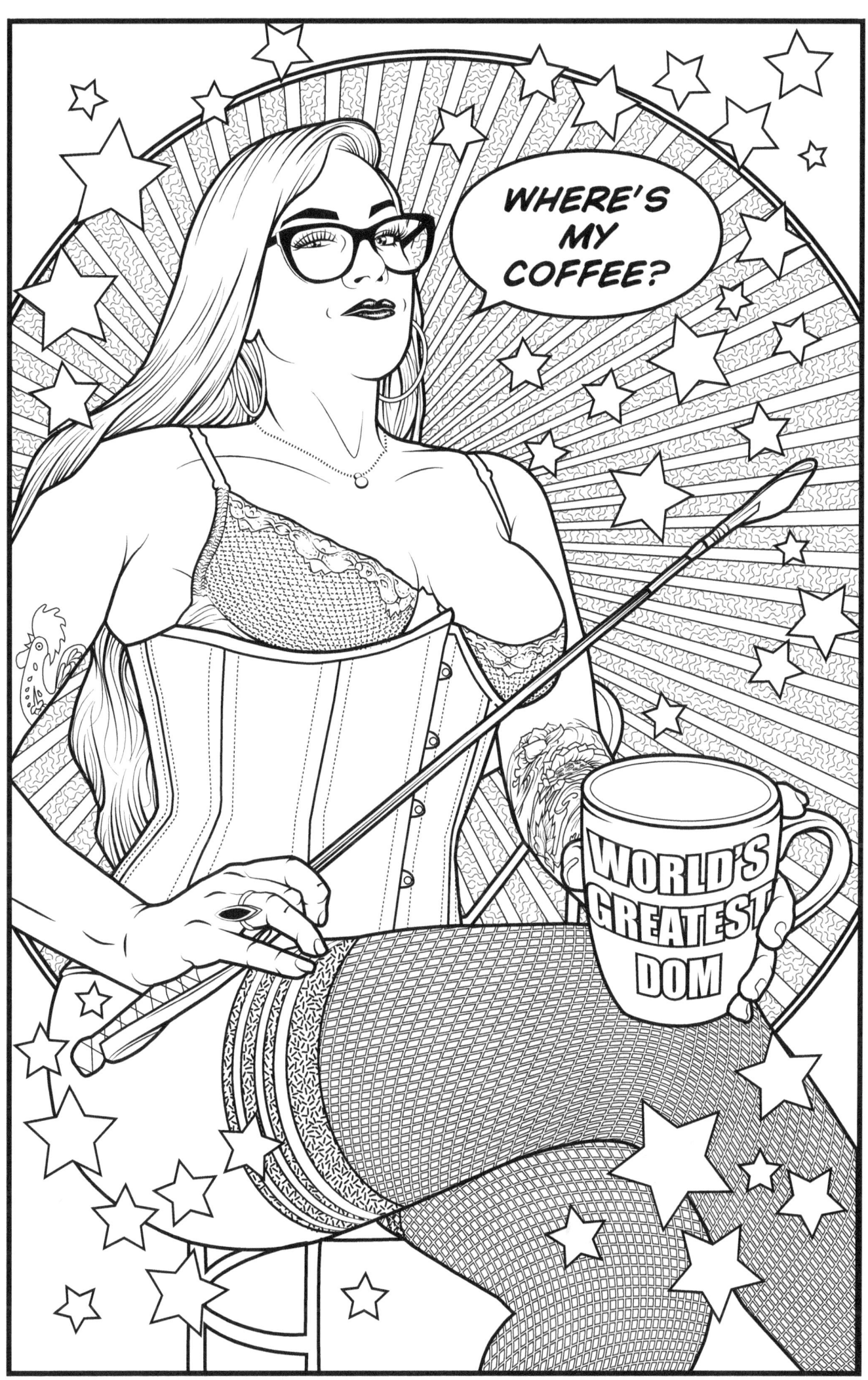

Muza's Back

Models: Muza de la Luz

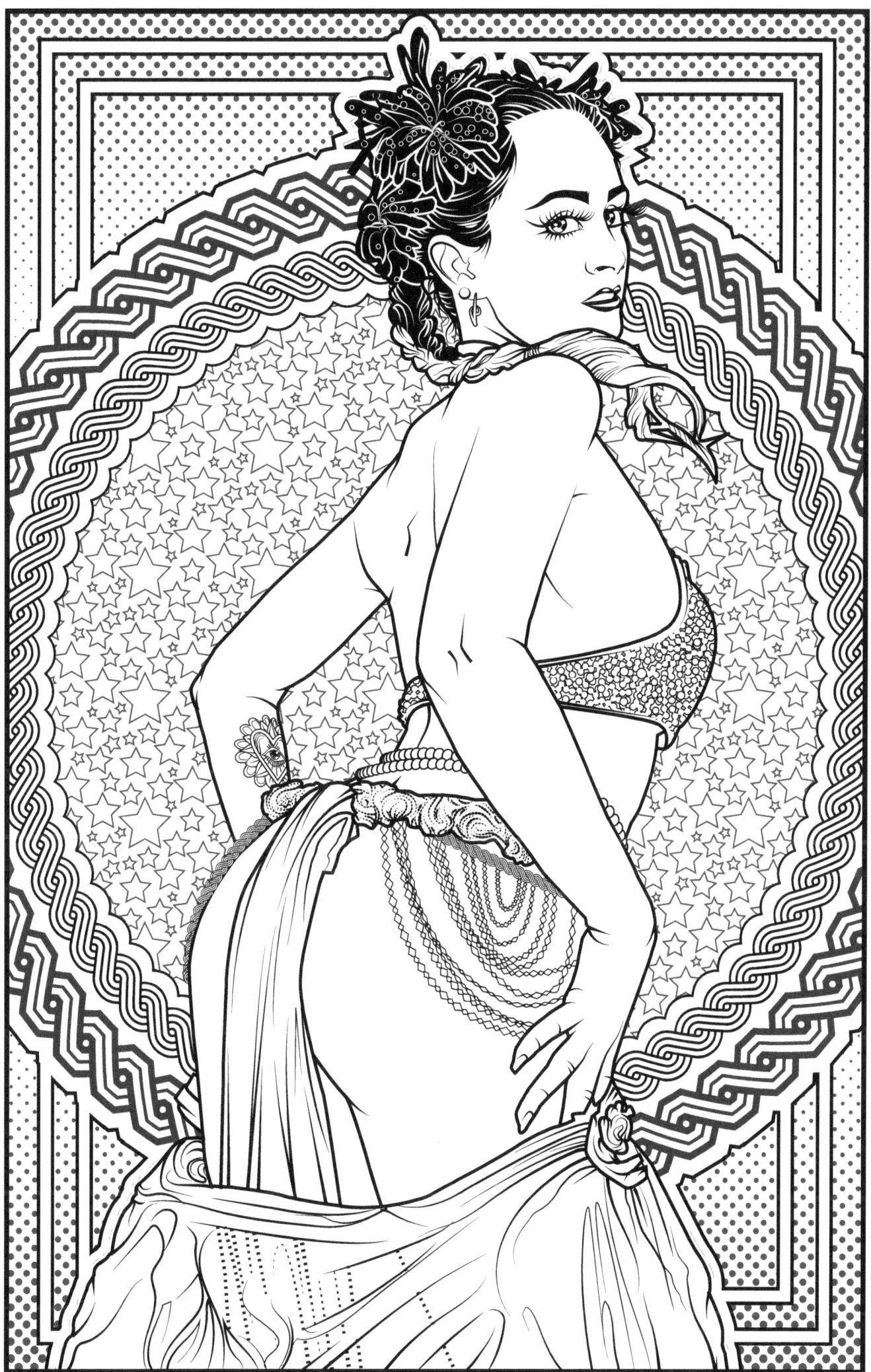

Release The Quacken

Model: Ellie Kimiko

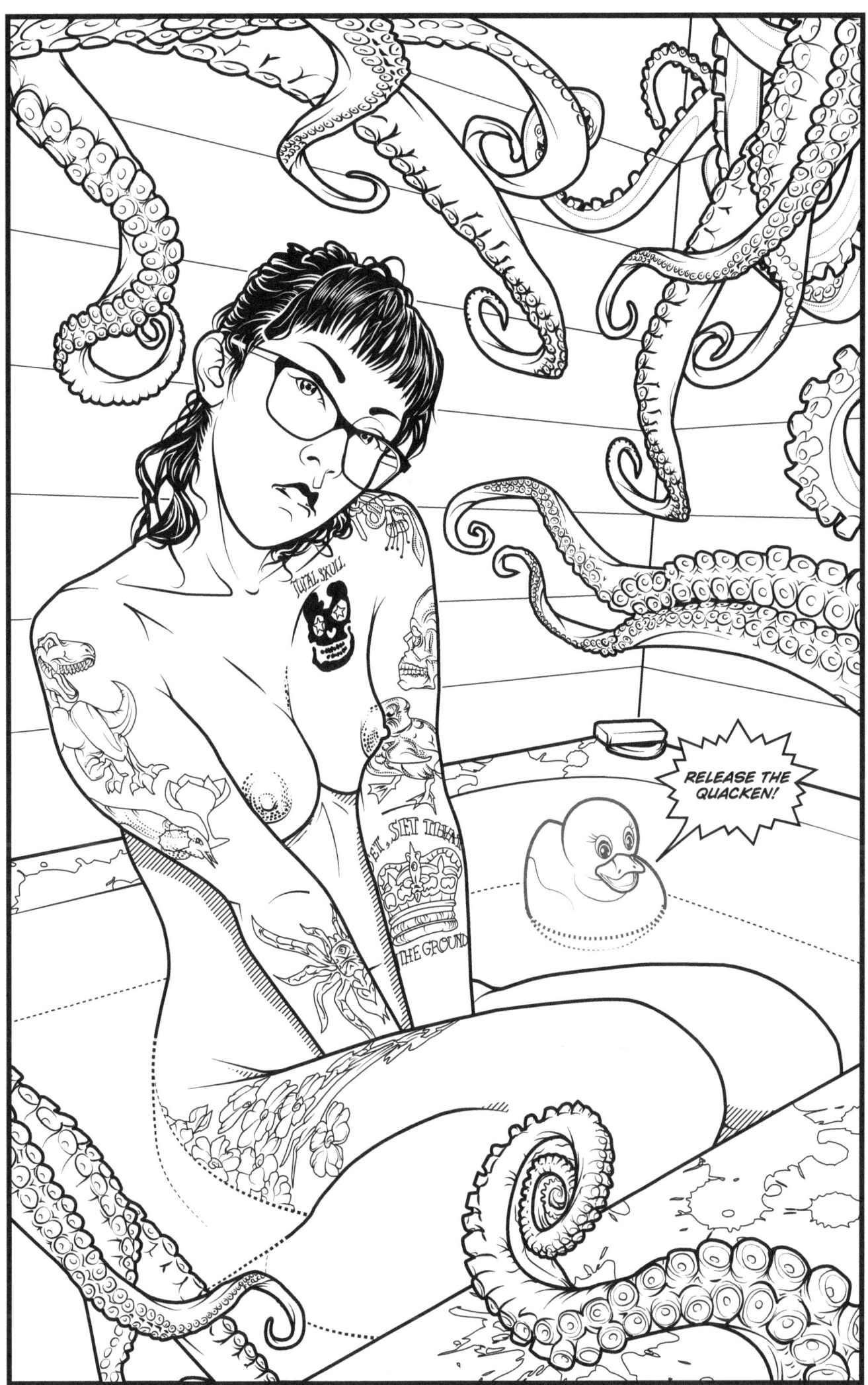